Beating The Odds:
A Story Of Survival

Beating The Odds:
A Story Of Survival

Isaac Crawford Jr.

To order additional copies of this book, contact:
Xlibris Corporation
1-888-795-4274
www.Xlibris.com
Orders@Xlibris.com
68030

Contents

Prologue 7

Childhood in Illinois and Alabama 15

Move to Tuskegee 33

Another Move 37

Isaac, Jr. 43

Family History July 3, 1996 75

Mobile and Tuskegee Revisited.. 77

The Rest of The Story... 81

Politics.. 116

Prologue

This documentation of the Crawford-Wright family started in the mid 1980's when personal computers became a replacement of typewriters and offered many additional qualities. My daughter, Rosemary Crawford Smith, and I began to compile a data file of personal information and statistics pertaining to all known family members, and set up a family tree.

My Mother, Martha Jane Wright Crawford, suffered from severe memory loss during her later years preceding her death in 1989 and was unable to provide additional information not already gleaned in earlier times. But her scrapbook and family Bible provided some important facts and obituaries regarding both sides of the family. At family reunions my siblings, Peter, Ruth, Jerry, and Marie, waxed nostalgic about certain childhood events and recollections, often in conflict with the viewpoint of others. Peter said he was reminded of the analogy of blind people standing before an elephant and trying to describe it. One standing by the trunk would describe it as thin, round and very flexible. The one by the leg would consider it big and round like a tree trunk. Another by the side would describe it as flat, hard and wide. And the one by the tail would consider it as thin, short and flexible. All were correct but did not provide the total description of the elephant. In an effort to reach a consensus it was decided that each brother and sister would document their earlier years to the best of their ability and send it to me for arranging in chronological order.

This led to my decision to continue the documentation and to do additional research at city halls, libraries, and state and national archives to verify facts pertaining to slavery, wartime services, and geneaolgy. Additionally, I have continued to add personal family events and involvements over the years, weaving this into a story of overcoming the obstacles and difficulties of the great depression, segregation, physical health, and getting involved in many church and community endeavors for continued growth and enrichment of life.

This book is not intended to belittle or embarrass any family members or aquaintances. We all have our faults and flaws. While the truth is stated, many controversal details are left out.

It should also be acknowledged that while African is our dominant heritage there are American Indians (Cherokee in Kentucky and Seminole in Alabama), and a sprinkling of Irish ancestors on both sides of the family.

At a recent symposium sponsored by Friends of the National Archives one of the presenters was a DNA researcher who talked about using DNA to determine the percentages of race received from your ancestors. During a break I asked about the cost of this procedure as I was curious about verifying the accuracy of family legend. The $400 fee was something I could not afford during the current recession with its esculating costs of living, but maybe somewhere down the road it may be feasible.

Early Family History: Paternal Side

The earliest traceable ancestor from the Crawford side of the family is Caroline Crawford, born in Virginia in 1834. She was a 36 year old mother of seven children in the 1870 U.S. Census, living in Millers Creek, Estill County, Kentucky. According to family legend the father of her children was a full blooded Indian, but there is no name to trace. She lived adjacent to 65 year old Oliver Crawford and his wife, Delina, 58. In all probability she was a former slave in their household. The slave record of 1860 listed a 26 year old black female as part of his property. He probably provided land for the family after emancipation and she continued as his housekeeper.

Caroline's children were Henry, 21; Isaac, 19; Amanda, 17; Peter, 15; Milly, 10; Anderson, 8; and Will, 6. This means that she started her family at the age of 15. Caroline and sons, Henry, Isaac and Peter were found in the Estill County tax records from 1872-1875 as owners of a couple of horses and a cow. The last entry was Caroline alone in 1875. They were not listed in the 1880 federal census and the 1890 one was destroyed by fire. The children obviously moved to other counties or states, and Caroline either moved with one of them, got married, or died.

Peter, who was born on April 20, 1855, became a groom in 1873 at the age of 18 when he married a 20 year old young lady of Millers Creek named Emily Stagner, born December 21, 1852, whose parents were both born in Kentucky. Emily was a 10 year old when granted her freedom. A record of their marriage could not be located by the Kentucky Archives in response to a written request.

Kentucky was a neutral state during the Civil War and many of the residents fought for either the Confederacy or the Union Army. As a neutral state, the Emancipation Proclamation had no bearing. It only applied to the Confederate states. But Blacks could gain their freedom by enlisting in the Union Army, which Emily's father did. Archive files for Black enlisted men from Kentucky show two Stagners; Peter, who served as a private in the 12th U.S. Colored Heavy Artillery, and Archy, a private in the 56th U.S. Colored Infantry. That is all the information provided by the Civil War records, but the pension files provide much more information. Peter Stagner's widow applied for a pension in 1866 and a request form for the details was submitted to the National Archives in Washington, D.C. That 27 page file plus perusal of the slave schedule for 1860 provided the following facts. Peter Stagner was a 26 year old slave on the farm of his owner, Thomas Stagner in Richmond, located in Madison County Kentucky in 1860, Thomas Stagner died that same year. Four years later, on July 23, 1864, Peter enlisted in the Union Army and was mustered in at Camp Nelson for a scheduled three year term. His description was as follows: age 30; height 5 feet 3 inches; complexion black; eyes black; hair black; where born; Madison County; occupation; farmer. He served in Company C 12th Regiment U.S. Colored Heavy Artillery.

His wife Phyllis Tudor, was a 24 year old slave in the household of Hiram and Elizabeth Tudor in the 1860 Census. According to several affidavits filed in support of her pension claim. Peter and Phyllis weer married at the Tudor home by a gospel minister named Thomas Yates in the customary manor for slaves. Different affidavits give the year as 1858, 1861 and 1862. September 10, 1858 is the most common date. Owners and acquaintances testified that they has no children. So one can only assume that Emily was the product of union with another slave since she was born six years before he and Phyllis united.

There is a suspicion that the marriage affidavits were a collaborative effort to cheat the government as well as Phyllis. A subsequent file received from the National Archives listed two men, one of whom was a lawyer, had Phyllis place an x on the papers for the pension claim. It was illegal in that era to teach slaves to read and write. A suit was filed on her behalf but the military records reveal no results of the outcome.

Peter Stagner died in quarters in Paducah, Kentucky of gangrene of the lungs on February 20, 1866

Peter Crawford and his bride, Emily Stagner, settled on a farm located at 809 North Fell Avenue in McLean County, Illinois. (Fell Avenue was named after the grandfather of Adelai Stevenson, who was a presidential candidate in 1952 against Dwight Eisenhower.) Peter and Emily's ten children were: Ida, 1877; Jerry, October 1878; Lottie, June 1881; Rose Crawford Curtis, August 1883; Peter,Jr., February 1885; Charles, October 1887; Isaac, August 31, 1889; Mollie?(probably Mary Crawford Bragg, 1892); Caroline Crawford Williams, February 1895; and Milly Ann Crawford White, 1901. Several of these names were duplicates of Peter's mother, brother, sister, and of course, his own.

Peter worked as a farm laborer, in a cannery, and later as a teamster for his own business. Emily was a housekeeper. One of his brothers, Isaac, was located in the 1920 census, living on South Linden Street in Normal. He was a servant in the household of 27 year old Frank Sterling and his 22 year old wife, Helen. There is a photograph of Peter and Isaac and two of Peter's daughters, unidentified, that has been in the family for many years.

Isaac, Sr. who was named after his uncle, graduated from Normal High School where he was a track star, winning numerous ribbons for his sprint speed. He often recalled passing the grandstand and hearing a white yell out, "Look at that N—Run!" He lived and worked on the farm until drafted into the Army on September 27, 1918, near the end of World War 1. His basic training was completed at Camp Grant in Illinois. Later assigned to tending mules, he was kicked by one and sustained a fracture of the left shoulder which never healed properly and gave him discomfort for the rest of his life. He was discharged at Camp Grant on the 14th of April, in 1919 after six and a half months of service. Isaac, Sr. also suffered from Epileptic seizures, a condition he had since childhood. This plus the mule kick, led his brother, Dr. Peter Crawford of Chicago, to initiate a claim for a service connected disability a few years down the road. Dr. Peter had Isaac come to Chicago and paid for him to attend the Dillon States Automobile School to become a licensed chauffeur and to be his driver during his lucrative medical practice. Dr. Crawford and his wife, Gertie, who were both the same age, had two sons, Harold and Donald.

Early Family History: Maternal Side

On the maternal side of the Crawford family were the Wrights whose matriarch, Martha Sloane, was born in Virginia, where slavery started in the 1600's. In the next two centuries many large plantations developed harboring hundreds of slaves and breaking up families by selling and shipping spouses and offspring to other parts of the country. Also many of these offspring were sired by the owners, their family members or overseers of the plantation. Martha was the result of a union of her mother, a house servant, with the Irish overseer from St. Louis, Missouri in 1830. When the mother was about to be transported to Alabama with her new owners, reportedly, the father offered to take the baby back to St. Louis with him because she looked white. Her mother declined the offer and went with her new owners on a three month journey by oxcart to Camden, Alabama.

Martha, when she grew up, united with Claiborne Wright and produced eight children: Morgan, Ned, Holbert, Claiborne, Frank, Susan Wright Jackson, and Kate Wright Nickens, a half sister to the siblings and half white. Frank Wright was born December 27, 1872 in Camden and migrated to Mobile as an adult. He worked as a laborer in an ice house and a factory and a hostler (taking care of the horses) for the city according to the city directory, and a grocer for a short time before returning to working with horses for the city. In 1899, on October 19th Frank and Emma Duncan were boarders with a Lizzie Tolivar on South Bayou Street when they were married by a Reverend McRae. They had already had a son, Louis Dell, born May 22, 1897.

Emma Duncan was the daughter of Thomas Duncan and Sara (last name not known). Sara was the daughter of an Indian. Emma was born in Fowl River, Alabama on November 12, 1877. She had one brother, Thomas, and three sisters; Eldelins, Irine and Roxyanna. (The unusual spellings were probably the interpretation of the census taker).

Frank and Emma had six other children besides Louis: Martha Jane Wright Crawford, July 26,1902; Ernest Morgan, November 19, 1904; Joseph Franklin, September 16, 1907, a son, John, born in November 1909, who died in early childhood; Edward Thomas, February 24 1910 and Irma Mozella Wright Caleb, November 22, 1913.

For a brief time the Wrights operated a small grocery store on Bayou Street in Mobile and sold fresh fish daily. Excessive uncollectible credit soon contributed to the downfall of the enterprise. Emma, who had been a laundress earlier, began doing housework for other families, and Frank went back to the stables taking care of horses for the city. He sent for his widowed mother to come to Mobile and take care of the house and children. It was during this time that she told her young granddaughter, Martha, who was given her name, about her beginning in Virginia and the oxcart trip to Alabama. She was an excellent seamstress and created many nice outfits for her grandchildren. She tried to teach the skill to young Martha but without much success as she lacked the patience to pursue the craft and grew up hating sewing. She did however, enjoy hearing the stories of her grandmother's youth and later as an adult, continued to seek information from relatives and from her husband's family. Martha Sloane Wright at the age of 80 was still alive at the time of the 1910 census, so her death obviously occurred after that date. No death certificate was issued by the Board of Health to confirm the exact date. Property records for the Probate Court of Mobile reveal a deed transfer from the Clark family to Frank Wright on April 22, 1908. Martha Sloane Wright probably gave her son money from the sale of her property in Camden to make the purchase of 65 acres of farm and woodland in Bear Fork, an isolated rural area outside Whistler and about six miles from Mobile. City directory records reveal Frank Wright living at 416 S. Bayou Street in 1900 and at 420 S. Bayou Street from 1901 until 1912. The move to the country occurred after that.

Sara Duncan, Emma's mother, came to live with the family for a while following the death of Martha Sloane Wright. Her lifestyle was not very coompatible with that to which the family had grown accustomed, she smoked a corncob pipe constantly and was not too keen on cooking and cleaning. When the family moved to the farm, the kids assisted with farm work and Emma continued to do housework and laundry for prominent families in the area.

Many years later Joseph Wright (Uncle Joe, who was in his late 80's, told me that the family had moved to Chicago for three years from 1914 to 1917. Documentation of this has not been found. He said he remembered having his tonsils and adenoids removed by Dr. Peter Crawford, and how sick the ether had made him.

The oldest son, Louis, served in the Army during World War 1 and, following his discharge, married Adele and had one son, Louis, Jr.

Martha attended the Moody Bible School in Chicago, and probably stayed with her brother, Louis. The rest of the family was back on the farm in Alabama during the 1920 census, but Martha has not been located in the Chicago soundex. (Probably one of the many city dwellers who have not been tabulated over the years) Her father, Frank Wright became ill with the flu during a visit after the war and they made an appointment with Dr. Peter Crawford, a black physician with a reputation for successfully treating patients of all races and developing many of his own medications. In his office they met his brother, Isaac, who was also the Doctor's driver. This meeting eventually led to a courtship and culminated in marriage on October 1, 1921. Isaac was 32 and Martha was 19. The ceremony was performed by the Rev. Edward T. Brown. They moved in with Isaac's widowed mother, Emily Stagner Crawford, and three sisters at the family homestead in Normal, and Isaac worked for a time with a railroad construction crew.

His father, Peter Crawford, Sr. had died August 19, 1921 at the age of 66. He was walking home from Bloomington and, according to an article in the Bloomington Pantagraph, felt ill and asked a woman whom he knew if he could come into her house and lie down. He soon passed out and died. His death was attributed to heart failure and Gastritis. He was buried in Bloomington cemetary on August 21, 1921. Perusal of obituary notes found in Martha's scrapbook reveal that Peter's sister, Amanda Crawford Smith, was living in Gary, Indiana; his younger brother, William,in Burlington, Kansas :daughter, Rose Crawford Curtis in Peoria, Illinois, and daughter, Mary Crawford Bragg, in Kansas City, Missouri.

Childhood in Illinois and Alabama

Pearl, the first child in the immediate family, was born January 29 1923 in Normal. Seventeen months later, on June 25, 1924, I, Isaac Jr., was delivered on the kitchen table by an Irish Doctor who said, "It's a Baay!" (boy), a story told many times over the years by my mother. On my birthday. Perhaps it's only a coincidence, but I have been an early riser and have spent most of my life working in the kitchen.

Martha got along fine with her Mother-in-Law, Mother Crawford, as she called her, and picked up some of the family history regarding the Stagners from her. But relations were not always pleasant with Isaac's sisters, especially Caroline, who was very protective of her older brother, Isaac, who had suffered from epilepsy since childhood. They moved into their own place at 115 W. Cypress Street in Normal with Pearl and me, and resided there from 1926 to 1928. They went on an extended vacation at her father's place in Alabama in the summer of 1926. There Peter was born on August 10, 1926, delivered by a Mrs. Hunter, a midwife. He was named Peter after Isaac Sr's brother and father, and Frank after Mother's father. The family returned to Normal and lived at 115 W. Cypress until moving to Chicago in 1928.

Dr. Crawford was working with the government to secure a disability pension for Isaac and suggested that the family come to Chicago to help resolve the issue. Dr. Crawford and his wife, Gertie reportedly offered to adopt Peter, who was named after him and was a frail and sickly child. Isaac. Sr's response was "you can have them all for all I care"; But Martha said, "If I had fifty, I would love them all and take care of them as long as I could".

In Chicago, Daddy had a dog that supposedly was vicious and had to be kept muzzled and on a leash. One day while they were out walking the dog broke free and raced home. Spotting the animal coming and terrified, four year old Pearl and I, a three year old, dove under a loose board in the fence that separated the adjacent property and stayed on the other side of that fence until our father came home and retrieved the dog. Pearl and I used to sneak up the fire escape to the window of a woman in the apartment above who would give us milk and cookies. Mother was against us having any contact with this woman, believing that she had a crush on Daddy.

On Saturday, June 16, 1928 at 6:45 a.m. Ruth was born. She was delivered at home in the apartment by Isaac, Sr. following instructions from Dr. Crawford, who though present was too sick to perform the procedure. Ruth was born with what in popular parlance is called "veil over face", a piece of the amniotic sac which occasionally covers the face of a new born infant. Dr. Crawford died of Pneumonia a few weeks later on July 12, 1928 at the age of 44 and at the peak of his career. He had struggled against seemingly insurmountable odds to go to medical school, including the lack of adequate finances and prejudicial treatment by some of his white classmates. The following excerpt is from a column in a Normal, Illinois newspaper after the funeral and was in Mother's scrapbook.

"Peter Crawford, Jr., son of Peter and Emily Crawford of Normal, Illinois died July 12th 1928 in Chicago, Illinois. His dream came true to be a doctor like their family doctor driving about and healing the sick and afflicted, and he never lost sight of his cherished illusion. Working for his father assiduously during his youth he managed to go through high school and at twenty-one started out in the great world to fight its battles alone. In this brief sketch can only be mentioned the vital points of his career. The first five hundred he earned and saved were swept away through the wily schemes of a sco undrel whom he had trusted. He then went to Chicago and engaged to work for his board in the family of a gentleman who recognized his fine qualities and was good to him while he studied night and day to enter medical school. After he had entered and had become the equal in ability to any of the students(he being the only colored member of the school) the burden of race prejudice bore heavily on him, and he would have been crushed by it had not some English woman in the class stood out against the gross injustice. The officials seeing her merit (Out of the spirit of justice) advanced him until he rose to the highest position and led the clinic. Receiving his honorable diploma, he opened an office in Chicago and built up a large and lucrative practice equally divided between white and colored patients.

His successful life (all too soon brought to a close) demonstrates the evolution of a soul; and shows how it is possible for even the lowliest beginner to rise to honor and distinction by industry and stability of purpose in bringing to pass the dreams of his youth.

The Reverend Mr. Hall under whom Peter was converted at 15 years of age came all the way from the Pacific Coast to conduct his funeral services in Chicago and Bloomington. His aged mother still lives in her modest home at 809 N Fell Avenue where all of her children were born" F.A.W.

After about a year in Chicago, the family moved back to the farm in Alabama. On September 15, 1928, for one dollar and love and affection, Frank and Emma gave five acres of their land to their daughter, Martha Crawford. She and Isaac, Sr. put up a small house and they farmed their five acres as well as some of Frank's land. There were three family homes on the Wright estate. On the Western were the Crawfords. In the middle, in the main farmhouse, were Frank and Emma Wright with Edward and Irma still living at home. Around the bend southeast were Ernest and his wife Rosa Harris, whom he married August 12, 1925, and their children, Ernest, Jr. called Buster, and Eloise, called E Baby. They later had Wilbur, Thelma and Hilda while the Crawfords still lived in the area.

Peter's misfortunes continued. He became quite ill, was burning up with a high fever, could not eat and was losing weight rapidly. It appeared as if he was going to die. Peter claims that Mother told him this story, although it sounds like something from Alex Haley's book "Roots".

One moonlight night Martha wrapped him in a blanket took him outside and laid him on the ground. As the dogs howled she prayed to God to spare his life. Years later she said to Peter, "You are here today, so surely he heard me."

Irma was still in school She graduated from Dunbar High School in Mobile in 1931. Edward worked part time for other farmers and dairies in the area. He used to roll his own cigarettes and Buster and I would sometimes pick up the discarded butts and pretend we were smoking. Friendly rivalry often took place between Buster and me who were about a year apart in age. One game was to stand in the gravel lane that served as a roadway about fifty yards apart and hurl stones at each other. Luckily we were agile enough to dodge the incoming missiles and neither suffered any serious injury.

Because the farm was about two and one-half miles from the nearest school in Water Works, Pearl did not start school until I was six and could accompany her on the trail through the woods. The village of Water Works contained the treatment plant for water for the city of Mobile. There were sufficient black families in the area to have a one room, one teacher school for six grades. Pearl and I had been taught how to read and write and do simple arithmetic by our mother prior to attending school. We used to do arithmetic with a stick in the sand out in the yard. As a result we spent a few months in the first and second grade and were promoted to the third grade at the end of the first year. We were often picked on and chased by older kids after school who apparently resented our scholastic ability. The teacher for the first few years was a Mrs. Powell, a strict disciplinarian who frequently made children go out into the yard and break off switches from brush to be used for spankings, and sometimes used rulers on the hands of offenders. Students were seated in rows according to grade levels with the first grade up front and the sixth grade in back. One of the limited advantages of the one room system was the exposure to information from all grade levels. Perhaps the greatest drawback was the time constraints which prohibited greater in depth and detailed work and practice. One had to have a thirst for knowledge and do much of the work on your own at home at night after all the chores were completed.

On January 5, 1931, Mother gave birth to fraternal twins. They were delivered at home by the same midwife, Nora Hunter, who had assisted with Peter's birth in 1926. Jerry was born first and weighed five pounds. Marie weighing about eight pounds was delivered about a half hour later. The size differential persisted into adulthood. Upon hearing their cries throughout the house, I, at six and 1-half years of age, asked Daddy where they had come from. His response was, "Didn't you see the stork? He just left". Whereupon, I dashed outside and looked skyward to see a large vulture (buzzard as we called them) circling overhead.

The youngest three children, Ruth, Jerry and Marie all had freckles and red hair which they retained. Supposedly, Pearl, Peter and I were born with reddish hair but it turned darker in early childhood. Martha and most of her siblings had grey eyes, further testimony to the Irish genetic input.

Martha wanted her children to use the more formal title, "Mother" when addressing her. Naturally, as infants, pronouncing the "oth" of mother was beyond our capabilities, so the resulting name came out "Mudder". This habit became so ingrained that even as teenagers and adults some of us still called her "Mudder", and were embarrassed as siblings would burst into laughter. Deeply religious, Martha was never heard to curse or utter profanity, although the tone in which she spoke when angry certainly sounded like it. When upset at some of our shenanigans she would say, "Oh Blubbie Shubbie"! If really perturbed, she would say in a disgusted voice, "fiddlesticks and ham sandwiches!" She sometimes said, "Go to Halifax"!, which the children thought of as "Go to Hell" and were surprised when we discovered in Geography that there really was a place in Canada called Halifax. She would occasionally discipline us, but this task was usually left to her husband. When he went overboard with too vigorous a thrashing, she would try to intercede with, "Now Daddy, that's enough!"

Isaac Sr. had a facial tic and was very sensitive about people staring at him. During supper one evening he caught Pearl staring at him and bellowed, "What are you looking at?" To which she meekly replied, "Looking at you looking at me," He frequently used derogatory nicknames for the kids. Ruth was "Topsy" I was "Elephant Head." Marie was "Pest". His favorite quote to anyone even suspected of misbehaving was, "I'll knock you through that wall, you skunk head ape you". Generally his bark was worse than his bite, but there were moments when he went overboard.

A telegram was received on November 24, 1932 from Daddy's sister, Caroline, stating that their mother, Emily Stagner Crawford, had died and to wire if coming for the funeral service. The telegram was sent to our post office box 95 in Whistler and was received when Mother drove into town to pick up the mail. Following discussion at home, Mother and I went back into town to send a reply that they would not be able to attend the funeral. Emily had been a resident of Normal for 57 years, since she and Peter had moved there from Kentucky in 1875. She was a month shy of 80 at the time of her death. Contributing factors to her demise according to the death certificate obtained many years later were Hypertension, Arteriosclerosis and Myocarditis. Her father is listed as Peter Stagner and her mother as "unknown". (Ironically, this certificate lists her race as "White" despite the fact that she was 100% Black all of her life. Communication with the office of the state of Illinois for correction resulted in them saying that they couldn't change the data. Funeral services were conducted at the Trinity Baptist Church by the Reverend William Pankey and she was buried in Bloomington Cemetery.

At the conclusion of the school year in 1933, our parents decided to return to Normal, Illinois. Trading in the Model A ford for a 1929 Essex, they packed and drove through Alabama, Mississippi, Tennessee and Kentucky to Normal where they rented a house at 115 Walnut Street. I recall a scheme we encountered in Mississippi where local farmers would flood sections of the unpaved road and charge drivers for pulling them out of the mud with a team of mules. The price was quoted as "2 bits" or "4 bits". That was the colloquial term for quarters I later learned. Another experience I witnessed was my parents having to go to the side or back door of a food establishment to get take out food for us to eat in the car.

Caroline Crawford Williams, her husband, John, and three children, Clyde, Bobby Jean and Donald lived at the Crawford family homestead on Fell Avenue, so we cousins got to know each other. Another sister, Rose Crawford Curtis had a son, Jack, who was attending the Normal branch of the University of Illinois and was a track star. Jack Curtis was a frequent visitor to Walnut Street, especially when Mother's sister Irma, came for an extended visit. Mother took in some college students as roomers to supplement the family income. In nearby Bloomington lived Isaac's brother, Jerry and his wife, Nezzie, at 504 S. Madison St. Jerry was a washer in a laundry and his wife was a housekeeper and provided rooms for several boarders. Also in Bloomington were sister, Mary Crawford Bragg and her husband, Thomas, who worked for the baggage department of the railroad. As an employee, Thomas was permitted to ride the train free of charge. He looked white and could escape the prevailing "Jim Crow" treatment of the South when visiting the family in Alabama—as long as he left his dark wife home.

John Williams was a custodian in a local movie theater where Pearl and I would sometimes go for a nickel each. John frequently used to make a concoction in his kitchen of raw eggs, oysters and catsup, and slurp it down to the amazement of us watching children. I became sick after eating some oyster stew and have never eaten oysters since. A nearby dairy sold skim milk for 12 cents per gallon if you brought your own pail, so that was the source of milk for the family. A supermarket called the Piggly Wiggly was only a few blocks away for grocery shopping. The railroad tracks were also not too far away and it was exciting for us to go watch the trains go by, wave at the engineer and fireman, and observe the people through the windows of the dining car.

The house had a cellar with a coal furnace and a coal storage bin that was filled by a chute through the cellar window. There was snow to be shoveled from the walks during the winter months. I have a picture Mother took of me at the age of eight with a snow shovel in the back yard. One morning while Daddy was shoveling the front sidewalk, the young daughter of a white family that had recently moved on the street from Kentucky stopped and stared and finally asked, "Y'all got any pick-a-ninnies at y'alls house?" During heavy downpours of rain, the flat street was flooded and water sometimes rose as high as the top cellar step and had to be pumped out afterwards.

Pearl and I were in the fourth grade attending an integrated school for the first and only time during our childhood. We were very self-conscious and aware that all eyes were on us when the white teacher discussed slavery, Abe Lincoln and the Civil War. I received a certificate in June for the number of books I had read. The certificate is still in my file. Peter was in the second grade. Ruth started kindergarden until it was discovered that she was underage and had to drop out. The school was close enough for the children to go home for lunch instead of having to take a bag or pail as we did for the two and a half mile romp through the woods in Alabama. Peter's teacher would read portions of a story to the class near the end of each school day. He vividly remembers the reading of "The wizard of Oz".

Roller skates were given to Pearl and me and we became quite proficient in skating up and down the sidewalk. Occasionally Daddy would adjust a pair with the skate key to fit Peter, who almost invariably, would end up on the ground. So he bought Peter a little red wagon with a long handle. With one knee on top of the wagon and one foot on the ground, Peter would push himself along the sidewalk. Fireworks were legal then and all the neighborhood children were shooting off firecrackers, sparkles and rockets. One boy tossed a six inch lit firecracker toward me. I threw up my hands just as it went off and suffered blackened, sore and swollen fingers.

All of us children came down with Chicken Pox and were quarantined for a time. It was worse for the twins, Jerry and Marie, who suffered scars from the itching and scratching. Daddy and a friend were frequent checker players and during the excitement of a close game the friend would keep shifting his chair. Eventually he would end up with one leg of the chair falling into the floor grate of the heating system.

Finally realizing that Illinois was too expensive for them even though Isaac Sr. had received an increase in his pension and a back bonus, the family returned to the farm in Bear Fork and seriously tried to make a go of it. The house was enlarged by enclosing the porch to make a new bedroom and building a new porch. They bought a ten acre plot on the North side of the house making a total of fifteen acres and began raising chickens, pigs and cows and growing cotton, corn, peanuts, sugar cane, sweet and white potatoes, Okra, tomatoes, carrots, string beans, turnips, strawberries and watermelon. Over the years the family had horses or mules for the farm work. One memorable horse was a female bronco that would frequently run wild while pulling the plow or wagon. Unable to control her, Daddy sold her and later ran into the man who had bought her. He said the horse was gentle as a lamb. He had bred her and it made a world of difference in her behavior. A later male horse became ill with an infection and eventually died. I was given the task of digging a hole big enough to bury him. Grandpa, Frank Wright, frequently used to load produce on his wagon and peddle it in Whistler. I, and sometimes other siblings, often accompanied him on these expeditions as he drove slowly through the streets calling out the names of fruits and vegetables for sale. One year there was a bumper crop of sweet potatoes in order to preserve them for future use during the winter, a hole was dug below the shallow Alabama frost line and lined with straw. Potatoes were placed in the hole, covered with additional straw and the soil replaced. Somehow a band of wild pigs discovered this inviting repast and devoured most of the sweet potatoes before they were spotted and chased away.

On August 18, 1934, Edward Wright married Barbara Kiel, a girl from a small farming community called Orchard. Edward and Barbara moved into the barn adjacent to the Wright family home after converting a portion of it to living quarters.

Back in elementary school in Water Works, Peter and I and a couple of other boys went to the assistance of the new teacher, Mrs. Houston, whose car would not start. We pushed it, and when she engaged the clutch with the ignition on, the engine fired up. Jumping on the running boards, Peter and I rode down the hill until the car approached the trail through the woods which would carry us home. There we jumped off, not knowing that our bodies were still traveling about 15 miles per hour, the speed of the car. Tumbling and sliding across the gravel shoulders and gullies, we suffered painful scrapes and bruises—an early lesson in Physics.

Mrs. Houston initiated a social program whereby she, the students and their parents, visited each other's homes during the school year. The small enrollment in the school made this experiment feasible. Especially enjoyable for the students was the fact that a snack and beverage, usually lemonade, were served.

There were several brooks and an eight mile creek to cross getting to and from school. Our father would cut down trees, trim the branches and use the logs as a bridge across the small streams, anchoring them with stakes driven into the ground at each end. The county maintained the bridge across the creek which was more like a small river. The planks were separated by several inches and there was no railing. During heavy rain the water sometimes would rise over the planks, making crossing dangerous or impossible.

School Lunches were carried in a brown paper bag or in a one gallon syrup bucket with a lid. Syrup buckets were also used as water buckets, bait pails, a tadpole aquarium and as a bathroom accessory at night, especially during the winter to avoid going out in the chill of night. Obviously, different pails were used for these varied activities.

Although there was m much work to be done on the farm—taking care of the animals, planting, weeding and harvesting, getting wood for cooking and heating, getting water from a spring until a well was dug, milking the cows, etc.—Peter, Buster and I managed to find time to engage in recreational pursuits, especially during the summer. We went swimming and fishing together and trampled through the woods to the creek barefooted in spite of rattlesnakes and moccasins in the area. Uncle Ed introduced us to swimming in the creek by teaching us how to do the dog paddle and eventually how to roll over and float on the back. At first we would find a shallow spot and crawl along with our hands touching bottom, kick our legs on the surface and yell to Uncle Ed, "Hey! I'm swimming". At which point he would often pick us up and throw us into deeper water and laugh as we struggled and panted to reach an area where we could stand up. We swam nude in that isolated spot. The butcher at a meat market in town would often give us animal kidneys which we would use as bait for catfish, setting poles at various spots along the creek and returning the next morning to retrieve our catch. Usually there were several catfish, but on occasion, we would pull in an eel, a turtle, or a snake. Some afternoons we would gather worms or catch grasshoppers to use as bait for trout and perch. The first eel that Peter pulled in was mistaken for a snake and he was ready to throw away pole, line and all until Grandpa Wright convinced him that the eel was edible and not harmful at all. Prankster, Uncle Ed, told us that the proper way to kill an eel was to beat it on the tail because that was where the brain was located. It was sometimes startling when cooking catfish to watch the muscles twitch when they hit the hot fat.

One day on the way to the creek for swimming, we passed a field with ripe watermelon and decided to swipe one and cool it off in the creek while we swam. Imagine our disappointment when we heaved it into a deep pool of water at a bend of the creek called the Black Gum Hole only to have it sink beneath the roots of overhanging trees and never surface.

On another occasion, two boys from Whistler were visiting with their family and joined us at the creek. Since they could not swim, they were warned not to go into the deep part. After a while one of them jumped in over his head and began yelling and flailing in panic as he bobbed up and down. Playing the hero, I dove out to rescue him and was instantly grabbed around the neck in a viselike grip by the terrified youth who tried to climb on top of me. As we both began to sink, Peter was able to pull the boy off and toward shore. Choking and gasping for air, I was able to grab hold of a log that lay across the creek and eventually was sufficiently recovered to slowly struggle out.

Several abandoned plots on the way to school where homes had been destroyed by fire had fruit trees and berry bushes still producing. Walking home from school one afternoon, I decided to sample some pears ripening on a nearby tree. Climbing up, I was reaching for the inviting fruit when my uncovered head encountered a hornets nest. Receiving several stings on the top of my head, I fell to the ground, and luckily, sustained no other injuries.

Living in virtual isolation in the country, we children had no awareness of the true extent of our poverty. We assumed that most people lived like that. No electricity was available and kerosene lamps or the glow from the fireplace were used for nighttime activities and reading. Cooking was done on a wood burning stove. Hot water was made in a tea kettle or pot on the stove, or in a large black kettle outdoors for laundry. A pot bellied stove in the living room supplied heat for cool winter nights and was a favorite dressing room in early morning as children gathered around it. There was no bathroom. An outhouse provided toilet facilities, with Sears-Roebuck catalogs, or some similar publication serving as toilet paper. When the hole underneath was sufficiently filled the small outhouse would be moved to a new location, the old hole would be sprinkled with lime and covered with soil. To take a bath, a small round tub would be placed in the center of the room and enough water poured in to wash up and rinse. Then the tub had to be carried outside and emptied. Saturday night was the usual bath night and the children frequently used the same water.

For all the cooking and heating a large quantity of wood was necessary. Daddy would cut down a number of trees and chop them up, Peter and

I were usually responsible for getting the wood to the house by placing it in burlap of feed bags and hauling it on our backs. The younger children were frequently involved in stacking the pieces.

Entertainment and news were provided by a small battery operated radio. Popular shows in the early evening were Amos and Andy, Lum and Abner, George and Gracie Burns and Jack Benny and Rochester. Especially memorable were the Joe Louis fights in the late thirties when the relatives would come by and eagerly await the outcome.

Late one afternoon at supper time, the Wright house about a quarter mile away across an open field, was seen in flames. There was no way to put it out. No fire department was nearby, and if there had been, contact could not have been made in time. A bucket brigade for a fire of that magnitude was out of the question, so everyone watched in horror as it burned to the ground. The grandparents stayed with us that night and later moved into the barn which had been converted into living quarters for Edward and Barbara.

According to family history and my recollection, Frank Wright died May 12, 1936. A death certificate obtained from the vital statistics section of the Mobile County Health Department lists the date as May 1, 1938. Both accounts had him 65 years old. Frank suffered from asthma for many years and lated developed heart trouble. The cause of death is listed as Cardio-Renal Disease. Following embalmment his body was bought back to the farm and lay in the living room until time for the funeral. We children were usually taken to all funerals of relatives and church members in the area, and I grew up associating the aroma of cut flowers with death.

On June 1, 1936, Pearl and I graduated from the Water Works Elementary school. I was valedictorian and Pearl was salutatorian. Sounds impressive until it is mentioned that there were only four students in the graduating class. My speech was written by Mother and began, "Friends and classmates, today we stand at the crossroads of life". After graduation, Mother took a picture of 13 year old Pearl and me, a few weeks short of my 12th birthday. We were standing under the rose covered archway in our back yard and it was one of the few childhood pictures. My outgrown jacket was about two sizes too small. The sleeves only came about halfway down my forearm.

That Fall we entered high school at the Mobile County Training School in the town of Plateau, located near a paper mill which created an awful stench when the wind was in the wrong direction. To help defray the cost of driving to and from school which was about 11 miles away, Mother picked up a student passenger or two in whistler in her 1932 Chevrolet. I frequently rode on the running board of the car, hanging on to the door frame through the open window. Seat belts and safety laws were not yet in vogue. In the "Separate but equal" (ha-Ha) segregated school systems of that era, there were no busses for black students, only for whites. Peter and Ruth had spent their first few years of schooling at Water Works, but when Pearl and I started high school, all the children attended Mobile County Training School which had an elementary wing. Jerry and Marie began their first grade class and wore blue and white uniforms.

Jerry, Ruth and Marie frequently played with their cousins of about the same age: Wilbur, Thelma and Hilda, children of Ernest and Rose Wright. Games such as hide and seek, hop scotch, bounce the board, jacks, pick up sticks and checkers were some of the favorites. A tire on a rope attached to a tree provided a swing; and a long plank secured to a wooden horse was a see-saw. Ruth and Marie made dolls out of grass and clay and used rags to make doll clothes. The foundation of the house was on wooden blocks about 18 inches high and provided an excellent place for the kids to hide out and play during hot summer days. The roof was covered with tin which was very noisy during a cloudburst and rusted very easily.

Irma Right got married on July 29, 1936 to Louis Caleb, pastor of the MT. Sinai Baptist Church in Whistler. Her mother Emma was a member of the New Light Baptist located on Route 45. Louis was quite an artist with wood carvings and used to make small manikins appropriately painted and attired to dramatize his sermons by depicting certain Biblical characters and events. With clever usage of pulleys and strings he was able to make these characters carry out the particular action called for in certain passages of scripture. (During a visit in 1975, though retired, Louis had the figures in his garage and had recently demonstrated on a local television show. I asked him to demonstrate the performance and videotaped it.)

I was baptized and joined Mt. Sinai at the age of 11 and became a Junior Deacon until the family moved three years later.

Ed's wife, Barbara became pregnant with their first child. When delivery time came complications arose because of her diminutive size. After two days of great pain, it was decided to take her to a hospital where a cesarean section was performed. The emerging child, Edward, Jr. suffered brain trauma and was never able to lead a normal life although he remained at home with his family.

As the oldest boy I was frequently punished by my father for many trivial activities especially disputes with siblings. One night while company was in the house, Ruth and I got into an argument—a normal childhood occurrence—and Daddy said, "I'll take care of you later". Dreading what was in store and unable to go to sleep, I was lying in bed a few hours later when he came into the darkened room and proceeded to flail away with a stick. One blow struck me across the forehead leaving a large lump that lasted for several days. This type of physical abuse ended when I was 12 years old, having worked since early childhood and now throwing around 100 pound bags of feed and fertilizer, I was quite strong for my small size. So on this particular day when daddy tried to hold me for a beating, I decided that I had had enough of this torture and refused to be held or struck. After about one-half hour of wrestling he was so exhausted that he gave up and never laid a hand, belt, shoe, or stick of wood on me again. In fact he tried to be buddy-buddy from then on, giving me a 22 rifle and showing me how to hunt and shoot with a shotgun. He neglected to tell me that a rifle bullet would travel about a mile and should not be shot on a level plane but aimed upward or down. One day I took a shot at a bird sitting on a fence and the bullet hit a tree over daddy's head about a quarter mile away. He took the rifle back.

Rabbits and squirrels provided an additional source of meat for the family but one had to be careful in eating in order not to chomp down on a pellet from a shotgun shell. Guns were a favorite hobby for Isaac Sr. He was constantly buying, selling or trading shotguns, pistols and rifles. His wife was certain that he was being taken advantage of in these deals—a view she often shared with the children.

Dogs of various description were part of the households in Bear Fork; an occasional hound for tracking game, but mostly assorted mongrels. Sometimes they would be bitten by poisonous snakes and would swell up and be very sick for a few days. No treatment was ever given and they either recovered or died on their own. One vivid memory is of a brindle colored male and a white female, Bruno and Flora, who frequently copulated in the yard and field as the entranced children watched, enjoying their birds and bees lessons.

White moonshiners often had whiskey stills hidden in the woods near Bear Fork and government revenue agents would frequently stop by and have Isaac Sr. sit in their car as they questioned him about the possible location of these illicit stills. I once made a coal kiln by piling pine logs lengthwise and covering them with soil leaving a small vent in front to light them and provide a small amount of air. The resulting smoldering, slow burn made charcoal which the moonshiners purchased as fuel for their stills. I also cut small trees for Mother's brother, Joseph to use as poles in his well digging business in Mobile. Uncle Joe would give me ten or fifteen cents when he came to pick up the poles.

Sometimes I accompanied Uncle Ed to the dairy a couple of miles away to watch him milk the cows. I would try milking a few, but invariably, after four or five milkings my hands would cramp and I would have to quit. Sometimes a cow would lift her foot and knock the pail over, or her tail would slap me across the face as she swatted at flies. Wages for farm hands were about one dollar per day in the depression thirties. and women who did laundry and housework for white families made about three dollars a week.

Grandma Wright worked for several families on the highway about a mile north of their property, bringing their dirty clothes home to wash and iron by hand. she carried them in a basket perched on her head. Two families names remembered were the Bellclappers and the Clarks who had about six hundred acres of farmland and woods. When Grandma sometimes worked until after dark, the grandchildren would go up the pathway to meet her. There was one spot on the trail referred to as" N—Head". When we inquisitive children sought the explanation for this title, we were told that many years ago a Negro had been lynched and his head chopped off and left hanging from a tree to serve as a warning to other Blacks who might be tempted to "Forget Their Place".

A Jewish family about a mile away to the east was very friendly with the Crawfords and shared in family events such as weddings and funerals; a practice almost unheard of in the prejudiced south. They had two sons who frequently played with Peter and me and once had shared some of their father's chewing tobacco. Naturally, after swallowing some of the juice, everyone was a little nauseous and dizzy. The parents gave me a young male calf which I raised as a pet, picking it up and carrying it around, feeding it milk from a bottle, making a little wagon for it to pull, and riding on its back when it got a little bigger. I was completely heartbroken when the calf was a year old and mother had Uncle Ed take it away to be sold to a butcher for meat.

Martha once ordered 500 baby chickens from a hatchery with the intention of starting a poultry business. A small chicken hut was set up for them with an oil heater to keep them warm at night. When the chicks were picked up at the freight office in Whistler, some of them had already died in the packing crates. Cannibalism and disease subsequently wiped out about half of them. It was soon apparent that the majority of them were males and egg production on a business scale was out of the question. So they ended up being slaughtered for meat especially Sunday dinner. The easiest method was to take a hatchet and chop off their heads on a block of wood. More fascinating, and certainly more cruel, was to take the bird by the head and swing it around and around until the head came off the body, and in spasmodic jerks, the body went flopping around the yard. Sometimes when a chicken was wanted for dinner, I would sit in the yard with the rifle and try to shoot it in the head so that the meat would not be messed up. Mother never wanted to be present when an animal was killed, but as soon as it was dead she would clean it and prepare it for cooking. She would go into the house and block her ears, especially when the squeals of a pig were heard. I once was assigned to perform this task for the first time and was quite shaken as the animal wriggled and squirmed and squealed in terror when I tried to slit its throat. No one had told me that the animal should be clobbered over the head to render it unconscious first. Appalling to us kids was the smell of wet feathers when mother would plunge a chicken into hot water for easy removal of the feathers.

In spite of his quick temper and sometimes erratic behavior as a father, Isaac, Sr. was quite religious; as was his wife. They neither smoked or drank alcoholic beverages. nor allowed cursing in the family. The typical punishment for a child who uttered profanity was to have his mouth washed out with soap. Peter was the recipient of this treatment on one occasion when about ten years old. In a huff, he threw some personal things in a bag and said, "I'm leaving!". To which mother replied, "Let him go. He'll be back when it gets dark". A few hours later Peter returned with tears in his eyes. That was one of the few times he was ever punished. His father said, "That's my boy!", and was never seen to spank Peter during childhood.

Most of the children were incontinent during early childhood and frequently saturated the sheets at night. The condition persisted longer for Marie and she was the recipient of cruel teasing by older siblings who called her "Polecat", the colloquial term for skunk.

Martha conducted a Sunday school class at home each Sunday before going to church. In addition to her children, five of the offspring of Brother Ernest were frequently in attendance. Family meals were shared together 3 times a day and grace was said at every meal. Sunday dinner after church was a big event in our household. Cooking and cleaning dishes were the major tasks performed on this day of rest. There was no card playing, dancing or going to the movies allowed. It wouldn't have mattered anyhow. None of us knew how to play cards or dance; and once in a great while, on a Saturday afternoon, mother would take us to a movie at a black owned theater called the Sanger in downtown Mobile. Chicken and pork were the meats most frequently served on Sunday—fried chicken or chicken fricassee with dumplings, and ham or roast pork. Accompaniments were sweet potatoes, macaroni and cheese or white potatoes, usually mashed, and greens of some sort: collards, turnips or cabbage. Lima beans and corn were also popular. Bread was frequently home made biscuits, rolls or cornbread. Cakes, cookies, pies and jello with bananas or fruit cup were popular desserts. A special treat occasion was home made ice cream. Although all the children were sometimes allowed to try turning the hand crank, the task of freezing the ice cream usually fell to me, the oldest boy. I would place a block of ice in a burlap sack and crush it with the back and sides of an ax and add the ice and rock salt to the tub around the canister of ice cream mix that mother had made. I would crank away until the mixture began to freeze and turning became increasingly difficult. The dasher would be removed and given to me to lick as a reward. Then more ice and rock salt would be piled over the canister and topped by a thick layer of newspaper until the mixture became solidly frozen. Everyone at the table had to recite a Bible verse after grace on Sunday. One very popular one, primarily because of its brevity was, "Jesus Wept".

One of my favorite tricks was to have Pearl call out to mother, "Isaac is in the cookie jar!" Invariably, she would say, "That's all right. He can have some". At which point I would reach in and help myself and even share some with Pearl. Getting to lick the bowl after cakes and cookies were mixed was also a treat.

Sometimes mother would let me mix the dough or batter. She also did quite a bit of canning of fruits and vegetables. and made jams, jellies and applesauce.

Christmas was also an important time in the Crawford household. Although the parents were more concerned with the religious significance of the event, we children were more interested in what we were receiving as gifts. For a tree, a large limb would be cut off a pine or cedar tree, placed in the living room and decorated. I would sneak out of bed in the dark and grope around under the tree feeling presents and trying to determine what I was getting. One year when I had requested a bicycle and felt wheels in the dark, I was certain that my dream had been fulfilled. Imagine my chagrin the next morning to discover that the wheeled present was a scooter for Peter.

Medical attention was practically non-existent except in life or death situations or serious injury. None of us visited a dentist in those early years. If a loose tooth needed pulling, a wire or string was placed around the offending incisor or canine tooth and tied to a door knob. The door would be slammed resulting in a quick extraction. For colds, chopped onions were mixed with sugar and the resulting syrup was spoon fed to the sniffling, coughing, sneezing child. An upset stomach called for baking soda dissolved in vinegar. Once I stepped on a broken bottle while running barefoot across a field and sustained a deep slash across the sole of my foot. The foot was wrapped tightly to stop the bleeding, and later, was cleansed with Grandma Wright's home made soap mixture of animal fat and lye and exposed to strong tobacco smoke. Antibiotics had not yet been discovered and probably would not have been available in any event. Miraculously, no infection occurred. Another memorable spontaneous home remedy took place when I got something in my eye while out in the yard. Rose, the wife of Ernest was nearby and came to my aid. Whipping out a breast, she squirted me directly in the eye with a stream of milk.

Martha took a midwifery course and was certified to deliver babies. This was a common practice in the rural South where doctors were frequently not available or affordable. She later delivered her sister, Irma's daughter, Delores in 1937.

The family sometimes visited Grandma Wright's relatives in Fowl River about 30 miles away: her brother Thomas, sister Roxyanna, and the family of Rose Harris Wright. It was in Fowl River that I first heard Ella Fitzgerald sing, "A Tisket, A Tasket ", a recording on a jukebox in a nearby store.

Sometimes on the way home we would stop at Bellingraph Gardens with its spectacular display of a wide variety of trees, flowers and shrubbery, brooks and ponds and aquatic birds. Another memorable trip was to Camden, Alabama, the birthplace of Frank Wright, where his nephew, Howard Smith, had a large estate and sharecroppers working for him. Mother had lived with them for a while as a child.

In our Junior year in high school, Pearl and I took a course in Spanish. One of the class highlights was learning and singing "My Country Tis of Thee" in Spanish: "O Patria Mia" The three verses are still remembered and sung many years later. I was also elected to the National Honor Society.

Peter was a playmate of the principal's son Clarence, and they often played ball after school while waiting for the upper grades to get out and mother to come pick us up. Clarence had an older brother, Benjamin, who was a troublemaker and made the mistake of challenging Peter to a fight, which Peter won.

Mr. Baker, the principal of the all black Mobile County Training School was a bi-sexual who had improper relations with many students of both sexes before they graduated. He seduced the girls and wanted the boys to sodomize him. Rumors had circulated throughout the school and community about him, but neither the white school committee nor the white superintendent of public schools took any action against this black principal who was only molesting black children. One afternoon, after lunch recess, I was rushing to class a little late and met him in the hallway. He walked over, felt my penis and asked, "You want to do it to me?": proof that the rumors were true. As a naive country boy, in shock and embarrassment, I quickly mumbled, "NO!" and dashed into the classroom. My parents, after hearing this story and fearing that Pearl and I might become victims of his erotic fancies, decided that the family would move to Tuskegee Institute at the end of our Junior year in 1939. There was also the possibility that we might be able to attend college there later.

Move to Tuskegee

So selling the farm and piling suitcases, six children, two dogs, a pair of bantam chickens and a family friend into the 1937 Ford, we set out for the 200 mile journey on a very hot, humid day. The friend was to return the car to the dealer. About half way through the trip, traveling at 65 miles per hour, there was a sudden explosion as an overheated rear tire blew out. As Mother applied the brakes the car swerved sharply and the other rear tire also exploded. Daddy, holding one of the twins on his lap in the rear seat, shouted, "Hold It Kid!" (his nickname for a wife 13 years younger than him.) The car spun sideways and rolled over twice down the highway, tossing Pearl out of the right front side onto the pavement. Flying glass, people, animals and personal possessions were strewn about when the upright car came to a complete stop on the side of the road. Mother was lying on her back on the shoulder of the road with her legs still in the open doorway of the car. Daddy landed in a ditch beside the road and suffered a dislocated shoulder; the same one kicked by a mule in Army camp. the shattered flying glass gave Jerry 3 lacerations in the top of his scalp with blood squirting upward and gleaming in the sunlight. The rest of us, wedged tightly in the rear seat remained in the car, along with Ruth who sat between Mother and Pearl up front. Shaken and dizzy, we staggered from the wreckage expecting the others to be dead. Miraculously, they were merely unconscious and with much moaning and groaning, began to regain their senses. Every one was splattered with blood, but Jerry was the only one severely cut. Luckily there was no traffic oncoming or directly behind the car to plow into the wreckage and increase the likelihood of fatalities. A passerby notified authorities and an emergency crew arrived and transported the family to a small religious hospital in a nearby town where the injured were sutured and patched. This was a rare occurence in the racial climate of the South, when many blacks, even years later, were left to die of their injuries because hospitals would not accept them as patients. (A famous example is Dr. Clarence Drew, a black physician who developed blood plasma during World War 11. He was involved in a crash in the Carolinas and bled to death on the highway because the powers that be refused to attend his wounds or transport him to a hospital.)

As I sat on the steps of the facility, a nurse came out and asked, "And how are you doing?" to which I replied, "My stomach hurts".

Surprisingly, despite being severely dented and having most of the glass broken, the car was still operational. New tires were installed, the doors tied shut and the trip slowly completed without further incident. One of the dogs was never seen again. The chickens were safe in their cages. Daddy was admitted to the Veterans Hospital for further tests and treatment. It was later discovered that he had sustained a fracture of the shoulder which calcified and further decreased mobility. Jerry was taken to John Andrews Memorial Hospital on campus for removal of his stiches.

The family rented a house in the village of Greenwood adjacent to the campus of Tuskegee Institute and joined the Greenwood Baptist Church, transferring their membership from the MT. Sinai Baptist Church in Whistler. Tuskegee Institute was a cultural oasis in the midst of the rigidly segregated south. There was a sizeable middle class of college administrator and professors, of doctors, nurses and administrators at the nearby all black Veterans Hospital and at the campus hospital. Numerous business and professional people in the community supplied necessary services. Movies were shown on campus on Saturday night and concerts and dramas were frequently presented. An art exhibit featured the paintings of Dr. George Washington Carver, who in addition to his many scientific discoveries in agriculture, was a respectable artist. Among the famous people who frequently toured the campus from this country and abroad were the Roosevelts. The President, Franklin Delano, came once and his wife, Eleanor, visited twice. One of her visits included a flight over the area with Captain Anderson, a black pilot and flight instructor. This tour led her to convince president FDR that a training facility for black army air corp pilots should be established at Tuskegee.

The town of Tuskegee located about 2 miles east of the campus was vastly different. It was run and controlled by whites, and blacks who shopped or went to the movies had to endure the humiliation of segregation. They had to stand in line while whites were waited on first in stores, and had to use a separate entrance and go up a flight of stairs to the balcony to see a movie. Students who wanted to go to Montgomery, some 42 miles west, or to nearby Georgia frequently hitchhiked to avoid the segregated busses. They knew that most blacks who came along would give them a ride.

My anger increased, and I found it difficult to comprehend how people could pretend that they were superior merely because their skin was devoid of pigmentation, especially when many of them were obviously inferior in mental capacity and physical condition. Years later, and after my contacts with many similar people in the Navy, I lost the proverbial chip on my shoulder and felt sorry for those people who had to resort to such desperate means to inflate their ego.

A nearby nine hole golf course for blacks was fascinating for Peter and me, and even more so when we discovered that business and professional people would pay us 35 cents a round to carry their bag and look for golf balls. I often caddied for Lt. Benjamin O. Davis and his wife, a beautiful redhead. Davis, a graduate of West Point was an instructor for the R.O.T.C. program at that time. He later joined the Army Air Corps and headed the all Black 99th Pursuit Squadron which was formed and trained at Tuskegee. He went on to become a famous general along with Chappie James, a Tuskegee graduate who was a Senior and in the civil air patrol during my Freshman year. (It seemed strange that Davis, in writing his memoirs many years later, never mentioned being assigned to the ROTC program. Perhaps he felt cheated. It was the custom in that era not to have blacks in charge of white soldiers.) Peter's favorite client was Mrs. Davis, who drove a yellow convertible. He also caddied regularly for Dr. Peters who was on the staff at the Veteran's hospital. Dr. Peters, a short rotund man, drove a small Austin Healy sports car.

At the end of the summer of 1939, Pearl and I began our senior year at Tuskegee Institute High School which was run by the college at that time. Peter began his freshman year. Ruth, Marie and Jerry attended the Lewis Adams Elementary School. Peter recalls having no books in high school because they had to be purchased. He tried to borrow books from his classmates during class to attempt making up homework that was assigned the previous night. This helter-skelter solution did not work and he was constantly behind in subjects that required extra attention.

I went out for football for the first time as an 132 pound senior and made the first team as starting center on offense and linebacker on defense. My one opportunity for glory came during a night game in Dothan, Alabama when I intercepted a pass and was headed for the goal line with blockers in front of me, only to be tripped up by an opponent already on the ground who reached out and grabbed my ankle.

I still liked to walk through the woods barefooted, and was hunting with a shotgun one morning when I approached the sandy bank of a small stream. About to take a step, I suddenly looked down into the open mouth of a cottonmouth moccasin as it reared its head at this intrusion into it's domain. Scared out of my wits, I whirled on my heels and dashed through the woods, never considering using the gun.

I had learned the basics of golf and been given some old clubs by people I had caddied for. So in the spring I signed up for a tournament for high school students. Noticing my absence from Economics class, the instructor asked Pearl where her brother was. When informed that I was playing in a tournament, the teacher asked how I was doing, to which she replied, "Great! He has the highest score".

Following graduation in May of 1940, there was no money for college, so Pearl and I found a variety of odd jobs. I worked on a coal and wood truck delivering fuel, as a dishwasher in a restaurant, and in a shoe repair shop, picking up and delivering shoes around the campus and village on a bicycle, polishing them and putting on the metal taps popular at that time.

Ruth graduated with honors from the eighth grade at Lewis Adams School on May 22, 1941 and was chosen to give the prayer at graduation.

Another Move

Always seeking new ways to improve conditions for her family, Mother learned of employment opportunities in New England for the summer of 1941 and accompanied several women from Tuskegee to the Berkshires to work as cooks, maids and housekeepers for wealthy summer residents. She worked for two spinsters in Salisbury, Connecticut, near the Massachusetts border, who were artists. She frequently drove them around the Berkshires and fell in love with the picturesque beauty of the area, especially Great Barrington. Arrangements had been made for her sister, Irma and daughter, Delores, to come to the Crawford house in Greenwood to take care of the family for the summer. Isaac Sr., went to the Veterans hospital in Illinois to try out a new medication that had been developed for epilepsy. Pearl went to Talladega, Alabama to enroll in a nursing program, and I, a few weeks from my 17th birthday, moved on the campus at Tuskegee to begin studies in the hospitality field, a course called Commercial Dietetics.

On a shopping expedition in Lakeville, Ct, Mother became acquainted with a Mrs. Banks, a black woman who had a summer home there. she also met the God Daughter of Mrs. Banks, a Mrs. Wiggam from East Orange, New Jersey who was visiting. Mother made a deal for a temporary residence with the Wiggams on Amherst Street in East Orange. She got a job as a home health aide, and later, worked at the Government Arsenal in Dover, NJ.

Irma closed the rented house in Tuskegee in November and sold the furniture to buy railroad tickets for Peter, Ruth, Jerry and Marie, and put them on a train at Chehaw for the trip north. Peter was given instructions for the change to be made in Atlanta and what train to get on and that Mother would meet them at the railroad station in Newark. Daddy went from the hospital in Illinois to East Orange. They later moved from the Wiggens' residence to a house on Halsted Street, one block away. The transition caused considerable difficulty in adjusting to a new school environment, especially for Ruth and Marie. Peter had attended an integrated school for one year in Illinois, but this was the first time for younger siblings.

I worked in the kitchen of the school hospital at Tuskegee that summer for my first internship. Commercial Dietetics was a five year program that could be completed in four by going year round. Each three months of classroom college courses was followed by three months of practical work in the culinary field (internships). That first year was extremely difficult. I was late paying my registration fees for the fall, had no money for textbooks, and received the grand sum of two dollars from home. The winter internship was done in the school cafeteria and allowed me to take a couple of additional classes. I also worked as a breakfast cook to help pay my room and board.

On Sunday, December 7, 1941, it was announced after chapel service that the Japanese had bombed Pearl harbor and the country was at war. The draft age was 21, so at 17, I wasn't worried about having to go fight. My optimism was short lived as the draft age was soon lowered to 18 and in June of 1942 I had to register and gave my home address as East Orange, NJ.

The summer of 1942 I worked as a cook at the General Hospital in Charleston, West Virginia, earning $15 per week. $12 was sent directly to Tuskegee to pay my bills and $3 was left to live on. I paid $1.75 a week for my room near the hospital and had a grand total of $1.25 for recreation and personal items. Meals were free at the hospital and that was the only place I could afford to eat. Near the end of the summer I received word that the family was planning to move to Great Barrington, MA. Having a couple of weeks off before returning to school, I joined them in East Orange for the trip to the Berkshires. The train from Grand Central Station would not be leaving until late afternoon so we took the subway to Bronx Zoo and had considerable difficulty in trying to determine which way was uptown or downtown.

In Great Barrington, rooms were rented from the Hamilton family until the Crawfords could get a place of their own. This was the final move for the family. They lived in Great Barrington from 1942 until 1978 when Daddy died; the longest they had ever resided in the same place. I worked for 2 weeks as a cook at the Berkshire Inn before returning to

Tuskegee. Peter began his junior year in Searles High School and Ruth repeated the ninth grade. Jerry and Marie were separated in school for the first time when she had to repeat the sixth grade and he went into the seventh at Dewey School. Peter worked for a time as a dishwasher at the Berkshire Inn and later as an orderly assistant at Fairview Hospital. He then worked for Reid's Cleaners until drafted in 1945.

In the spring of 1944, the Crawfords bought a two family house at 14 Elm Court, one block from main street and located behind the post office and Great Barrington Savings Bank. The duplex apartment next door was rented to the Smith family who became good friends as tenants and neighbors of the Crawfords. There were several dozen black families in Great Barrington and the surrounding towns of Egremont, Housatonic, Sheffield and Stockbridge. The children at home, Peter, Ruth, Jerry and Marie soon made their acquaintance and friendship as well as that of many of their white classmates in school. In short order they lost their southern accent and began to sound like New Englanders. Peter went out for football in the fall of 1943 and suffered a broken leg which necessitated making up the lost school work in the fall of 1944 and graduating in December. Jerry graduated from the 8th grade at W.C. Bryant School in June 1944. Ruth and a very close friend, Betty Gunn, went to Mary Potter Academy in Oxford, North Carolina for their junior year of high school, but returned to graduate from Searles in 1946.

After a difficult pregnancy in 1945, Mother gave birth to her Seventh child, Charles Edward, named after a brother on each side of the family. He was born on her 43rd birthday, July 26th.

Mother had worked as a cook in various homes and inns in the area and also began to do a little catering. With a baby to care for, she decided to open a Tea Room on Main Street in 1946. In addition to meals, it was a place for blacks to socialize and have parties. There is a picture of a birthday party for Ruth, celebrating her 19th.

She and Daddy had been Baptists all of their lives and with the assistance of others in the community, decided to start a church of that faith in 1944. The only Black church in the community was the Clinton AME Zion Church located directly across from their house on Elm Court. With the help of the Rev. H.M. Hutchings, pastor of the Alden Street Baptist Church in Springfield, whom they had met in New Jersey, an organizational meeting was held at 14 Elm Court with about 20 people in attendance. They named the church Macedonia Baptist and began in a storefront location in the same building block as her tea room was later established. With her missionary zeal, she soon had a Sunday School organized, a choir, Women's organization and a board of deacons on which Isaac Sr. served. He was also their first treasurer. They engaged the services of a part time minister. and became allied with the state organization, The American Baptist Churches of Massachusetts,TABCOM. Mother became active in the local subdivision of that organization, The Berkshire Baptist Association, and thus became acquainted with and friends of Rev, and Mrs. James Chase of the North Egremont Baptist Church. Rev. Chase participated in the funerals of our parents many years later.

Marie took piano lessons when she was 12 and 13 years old and wrote the class song for her eighth grade class at Bryant School. She also played for the Sunday school at Macedonia Baptist. During her first two years of high school, Marie was a star athlete, playing varsity basketball, field hockey and softball. She received a letter and a certificate in basketball.

When the Smiths moved out next door, in the late 1940's, Mother closed the tearoom and converted that side of the house into an inn and added a dormer on the back of the house. She also opened an employment office by enclosing part of the front porch. While she tried to provide employees for local businesses in need of workers, her biggest clientele consisted of teachers and students from the south who sought summer employment at various estates and inns in the area; a path she had followed which led to the final family location. Some students were perturbed about performing domestic chores, feeling that such work was beneath their capabilities even though they were desperate for money. Mother encouraged them to take the job for the summer. she told them, "It includes free room and board. You'll save more money. Just use it as a stepping stone. Work at it as hard as possible, then go to your chosen profession".

Martha Crawford was an eloquent speaker and frequently was asked to address different religious, social and civic groups. She was speaking on one occasion in Pittsfield when Mayor Capeless was heard to ask, "Who is that woman?". She joined the Order of the Eastern Stars and served as Worthy Matron of that organization. She also did quite a bit of outside catering, especially during the summer months, and often enlisted the services of me and My wife, Rosemary, There is a picture of me holding a decorated baked salmon at a wedding reception outdoors in Great Barrington.

The effectiveness of the new medication in controlling the seizures which Isaac Sr. had suffered most of his life allowed him to seek gainful employment, and he worked for a number of years as a chauffeur for a wealthy widow, and later as a custodian at the Great Barrington Library. Along with a change in health came a corresponding change in behavior. He exhibited more interest and pride in his children's accomplishments. This was a remarkable change from the day when I was discussing wanting to go to college and he said,"What do you need to go to school for? Get a job". When I worked at Williams College he would stop by on several occasions with the woman whom he was driving around the countryside, and also at the Log cabin Restaurant when I became Executive Chef. Jerry's completion of medical school and subsequent successful practice as a physician in Hartford was especially pleasing to Daddy whose brother had been a doctor in Illinois and his mentor and provider for a number of years.

He developed several friends and hunting buddies in Great Barrington and spent many happy hours hunting small game and deer in the hills and valleys around the area. I made the mistake of accepting the invitation to join the group on one deer hunting foray on a cold blustery day before dawn and never dreamed that we would spend the entire day until dusk, traipsing around the hills in South Egremont and standing shivering in various spots waiting for the elusive deer to appear. I never saw one all day. The cellar of the house was used for target practice with a 22 rifle and a pistol and usually involved competition against whatever son was home or visiting at the time. Needless to say Daddy was always the winner.

At the age of 70 he suffered a mild heart attack and was placed under medication for the rest of his life, but resumed hunting and other activities. He was the only male member of his family of four brothers to survive to old age. Charles died at 21, Dr. Peter at 44, and Jerry at 62. There is probably something to be said for bring the runt of the litter.

As Daddy's 80th birthday approached In 1969, the children discussed the possibility and planning of a family Reunion. Scattered over the Northeast from Boston to New Jersey and with our children growing up and starting families of their own, it was deemed desirable to establish some semblance of cohesion and contact. So Peter, Ruth, Jerry, Marie and I decided to schedule the first reunion In Pittsfield with Ruth as the host, and to rotate each year to each siblings location. Pearl had died in 1950 and Charles lived in a world of his own, generally not associating with his older brothers and sisters.

A picnic type cookout would start at noon and games such as badminton, horseshoes, croquet, whist, tennis and pool were often available depending on the various accessories present at each house. A large buffet dinner would be served and a birthday cake for Isaac, Sr., would be lit with candles and everyone joining in singing "Happy

Birthday". On that first reunion, Ruth hosted it at her father-in law, Charles Evans' mountain top retreat on the Taconic Range in Hancock, MA. A hilarious scene took place when the candles on the cake had been lit and just as everyone prepared to start the ceremony, up rushed Jerry's three year old daughter and blew the candles out.

The second one was held in 1970 at my one year old house in Dalton. Boston was the locale for the third at Peter's place on Supple Road. Then It was Foothills Way in Bloomfield CT with Jerry in 72. Completing the circuit was the 1973 reunion at Marie's place in Monmouth Junction, New Jersey. This tradition continued until the death of Daddy in 1978. Then it was decided to change the date to coincide with Mother's birthday, July 26. it is held on the closest weekend to that date. and has continued after her death in 1989.

A major change was made in the early 90's As the brothers and sisters began to age and retire, and their children had many kids who were grown or growing up and scattering. the grandchildren of Martha and Isaac, Sr. decided to accept the responsibility of financing and planning for the occasion. Rotation is still generally made among families of each sibling, but the affairs are usually held in parks or picnic areas for the afternoon and a restaurant or clubhouse for dinner. Some choose to go to a hotel or resort that provides everything on site. This allows everyone to be together for the weekend without having to seek separate accommodations, and makes for greater rapport and communication. Sometimes other events or tours are scheduled for Friday night and Sunday morning in nearby cities and towns.

Isaac, Jr.

All male students at Tuskegee were required to take R.O.T.C. for the first two years of college at that time (the early 1940's). The advanced program for the Junior and Senior year was optional. Chapel attendence was also compulsory. Cadets lined up in their respective squads, platoons companies and regiments in full dress uniforms and marched to chapel on Sunday morning. The religious service was enriching and enlightening. Dr. Richardson, the Chaplin, spoke softly and intelligently, and beautiful music was provided by the world famed 100 voice Tuskegee choir directed by Dr. William Dawson, who wrote or arranged many of the songs and spirituals sung by the choir. Vesper services on Sunday evening were also very uplifting. A full symphony orchestra provided outstanding music and a speaker of national or international repute provided a stirring message. On a few occasions, however, a Southern politician would express his bigotry views on race relations and receive boos from some students in the audience who were later chastized for their behavior toward a guest.

My second year in college was beset with financial problems as was the first. Again, without text books, I managed to squeak by in most subjects, having only flunked quadratic equations my freshman year. The shyness induced by years of isolated country living and lack of social skills began to diminish and a girl friend was acquired and I learned to dance and began to participate in extra curricular activities.

The internship for the winter of 1942 was begun at the Dixie Sherman Hotel in Panama City, Florida where all the cooks and the chef were students from Tuskegee. It was decided to terminate the program after about a month because of irreconcilble differences with the white dining room manager who was the girl friend of the owner and thought she should run the kitchen as well. Back at school, I completed the internship period as a cook for the newly formed Tuskegee airmen cadets, and suffered my second potentially serious accident. Working with a gas stove and oven for the first time, I was asked to light the oven. Getting a match, I Iturned on the gas and struct the match which went out. Going back across the room I got another match and tried again. Suddenly there was an explosion as the escaping gas ignited. Luckily, my head was not down to the oven. and I suffered no injury. The first accident took place during the winter of my Freshman year when I was standing in a watery spot next to an electrical outlet box operating a potato peeling machine. Reaching over to turn off the switch, my hand went into the circuit box instead and I was thrown across the room in a flash. For many years thereafter, I avoided handling any electrical equipment, even changing light bulbs.

In March of 1943 greetings were received from Uncle Sam ordering me to report to the draft board in Newark, New Jersey for induction into the armed services. The timing was good because a letter had just been received from the school treasurer informing me that I had to come up with the balance of my fees or leave school. Borrowing a few dollars from friends, I managed to scrape enough money together for train fare to Newark. Because of my R.O.T.C. training I fully expected to join the army and go to O.C.S. (Officers Candidate School) But a choice of service was only an option for volunteers, not draftees. When I appeared before the panel for assignment, I was informed that the Navy was looking for college men. They had just started taking Blacks in the regular navy in 1942. Prior to that time they had always been used as servants for officers: steward's mates and mess attendants. I would go to Camp Robert Small at Great Lakes, Illinois for basic training, but would have a nine day leave before reporting. Travelers Aid at the railroad station helped me call my parents in Great Barrrington for money to come home for the nine days of relaxation and socializing with family and friends.

In boot camp all trainees were restricted to the base until graduation from the eight week program of rugged conditioning. In the segregated, all black camps of that era, the commanding officer of each company was white and usually from the South since they supposedly knew how to handle Blacks. A chief petty officer, he had a black seaman first class assistant who bent over backwards to make life miserable for most apprentices. One day I was explaining to a fellow apprentice seaman how to perform various military maneuvers when the assistant yelled," 'Hey, you Knucklehead! You don't know nothing yourself. How the hell you gonna tell somebody else what to do?" So much for espirit de corps.

On a day when Henry Ford was scheduled to make an appearance, I became ill and fainted while standing on the parade ground for hours in the broiling sun. Taken to sick bay with a temperature of 103, I was diagnosed as having acute catarrhal fever and spent six days in the hospital. Even while sick I received the regular schedule of innoculations for overseas duty, Upon release a relapse occured and I was hospitalized for another five days. I also came down with the German Measles and was quarantined for a few days. So it was necessary to join a later company and graduate two weeks later than my original group. Over the years since, I have asked many doctors about Catarrhal Fever and none have ever heard of such a diagnosis. I have had a post nasal drip and excessive mucous production since that episode.

As a result of dental neglect during childhood, four of my molars were deemed beyond repair and had to be extracted. There was one bright side. For the first time in my life, I did not have to worry about money with free food, clothing and shelter plus $50 per month to spend as I saw fit.

After a short ten day leave at home I was placed on a troop train with many black sailors and shipped to a receiving station (Camp Shoemaker) in the desert outside San Francisco to await assignment. Liberty was granted every other day and we were encouraged to work for civilian companies during our days off base. I worked in a steel mill and a canning factory. On August 31, 1943 a large contingency of black sailors were assigned to a troop transport, the SS Mormacport, as passengers to New Caledonia, an island some 750 miles northeast of Australia. The trip took three weeks as they took an indirect route to avoid any possible enemy contact. Passengers were fed twice a day standing up around long tables in the mess halls. The ship was a converted cargo vessel and the cargo holds had been outfitted with tiers of bunks with about 18 inches of space vertically between each layer. Because of the heat and crowded conditions I spent most of the days and nights on deck. Unfortunately, spending long hours in the equatorial sun on deck without a shirt resulted in my first and last severe sunburn. When we arrived in New Caledonia after the three week journey all the skin peeled off my back.

It was on this trip that I wrote my first of three poems during my Naval time.

The U.SS Mormacport

From The Sunny coast of California to the rugged island of Caledonia, the SS Mormacport set sail. To fight through wind and sea and gale.

She sailed out of Frisco under the Golden Gate, loaded to the brim with men and freight; and a few Army nurses on the promenade deck, to add grandeur to the long ocean trek.

On she plodded through the salt and spray, dodging the Japs night and day; striving to keep alive the men who would help the allied drive.
To erase from the face of the earth. Japs who would regret their honorable birth

The island was a former French prison colony and the freed prisoners had settled there, establishing businesses, and many had intermixed with the darker natives called Kanakas, creating some very beautiful people.

New Caledonia was a staging area for men and supplies for the more advanced bases. Blacks had their own segregated camp and were assigned shifts for the 24 hour loading and unloading of ships and stocking of warehouses. Because of my training in the culinary field, I asked to be assigned to the galley, (naval term for kitchen) and became a first class seaman and a little later, a petty officer in charge of the watch, Ship's Cook third class. About a year later I was recommended for 2nd class but was informed that the quota alloted at that rank was full.

Lonely in a strange environment, many letters were written to family and friends in hopes of getting lots of mail. Many sailors spent their evenings gambling and I would watch and try to pick up pointers. I didn't care for rolling dice which was more luck than skill; but was fascinated by the strategy involved in poker and soon learned how to play. With open betting, what cards you hold loses significance in comparison to the psychology and bluffing which frequently determine the winner. Games would sometimes last until time to report for duty the next morning. Winnings exceeded loses and I was able to send money home during the 13 months spent on the island of New Caledonia and over the 2 remaining years elsewhere. Mother wrote that they were interested in buying a house and asked if a contribution could be made to the purchase price. About $2000 was sent over the next couple of years although my pay for overseas duty was only $ 96 per month. Of course I never mentioned to her that the money came from gambling, which she would have been totally against.

A pier alongside the bay provided a place for sailors to swim. One day I dove off into deep water and apparently went too deep. Coming up with pain in my right ear and loss of equilibrium, I staggered out of the water, then decided to dive in again trying to figure out what was happening. This only served to intensify the pain. A visit to sick bay revealed a ruptured ear drum. I was given a couple of aspirin (the usual treatment for anything that was not life threatening) and told to come back in about a week. After 5 or 6 nights of blood and pus on the pillow, things cleared up, no permanent damage occurred and hearing still remains excellent many years later.

An announcement was made that an exam could be taken by enlisted men for possible entrance to V12 school. This was a program in which those selected were given training and free education at Ivy league schools. I took the exam but was not given the results. Instead I was flown to Espirito Santo in the New Hebrides Islands, a receiving station, in October 1944, to join a group that had been shipped earlier. This first flight experience was on a C-147 with bucket seats placed along each side of the fuselage. With the constant roar of the engines and abrupt changes in altitude, it took 15 minutes to be able to hear again after landing. After a month there, we were shipped through the Soloman Islands, past Eniwetok, and on to Guam to join another black supply depot crew.

The usual schedule for cooks was from 1 p.m. to 1 p.m. the next day, with time off after supper until breakfast the following morning. Instead of this broken up daily routine, the crew decided to work a full day and have a full day off. So we would begin at 3:45 a.m. and work until after supper, with a few hours off in the afternoon. The next day was free time to relax, go swimming or tour the island which was 30 miles long and 8 to 10 miles wide. Although considered secure, it was not safe to go roaming the hills and caves looking for souvenirs. 7,000 Japanese soldiers were killed during the 4 months I was there. No major battles took place. These were mainly small groups hiding out and trying to ambush the Americans.

White marines and black sailors frequently had conflicts on many of the islands, usually over women. On Christmas Eve several Blacks returned to camp from downtown Agana after having been beaten by marines. About 50 Black sailors jumped on trucks to go retaliate. I tried to join them but there was no more room. Lucky for me because they were later court martialed and imprisoned. That night some marines drove past the hillside camp with a machine gun mounted on the hood of a jeep and sprayed the tents with bullets. Some rattled through my tent as I lay on my cot. Luckily, because the road was below the camp level the bullets went through the upper level of the tents and there were no fatalities or injuries. When the marines turned around to go back they were met with a hail of bullets and fatally wounded. The next day commanding generals, officers and guards searched the camp and confiscated over 300 weapons. Walter White, president of the NAACP came out to investigate when the Black sailors were court martialed. A little later, the marines were scheduled for the invasion fleet for Okinawa and many of them refused to go. In hindsight I can understand their plight. They were survivors of several other Island invasions and had lost many of their former associates who were replaced by new recruits. Black sailors stood along the roadside and cheered as these marines were marched at gun point to the waiting ships.

Once more I took the offered exam for V 12 school and was told by one of the yeomen (clerks) that I made the highest mark on the island. Again I was shipped out—this time on a British aircraft carrier bound for the states. It was many years later that I read that it was unofficial policy not to take blacks into the V 12 program. (Not a regulation or law, just a ("gentleman's aggrement")

It was while on Guam that I wrote my second poem; "Five Navy Men".

> In a tent exposed to all kinds of weather, five navy men are living together, a few rebels and a few yanks, full of fun and boyhood pranks.
>
> For two long years they have endured this rough, and at times the going has been quite tough.
>
> The mail has often been delayed, and trying to advance they have been dismayed.
>
> But still they labor and sweat and toil, longing constantly for American soil.
>
> And hoping and praying they will hear one day, the commanding officer proudly say,
>
> "Men your task over here is through. There is one thing more for you to do. Pack your gear in seagoing style. You will soon depart from this lonely Isle.
>
> Back to the states you men are bound; heading I'm sure for your old home town".

The H.M.S. Atheling was a small carrier to which a group of sailors were assigned as passengers. British cooks claimed that they did not know how to make coffee, the favorite beverage for most Americans, so I was asked to perform this chore. The flour on board was full of weevils and usually made into dark bread and cakes in an effort to hide their presence. The British laughed when we held bread up to the light in an effort to spot the bugs for removal.

The ship was near Honolulu on April 12, 1945 when it was announced that President Franklin Delano Roosevelt had died. He had been president from the time I was eight years old until almost my 21st birthday. I had grown from childhood to maturity with him in the Whitehouse. He was the first of modern presidents to reach out to minorities and establish programs that gave the poor some hope following the devastating depression that almost destroyed the country.

Back in California, I was granted a 30 day leave after 20 months overseas and took a troop train east. Two major events happened during this time off. The war in Europe ended on May 8, 1945; and a small plane crashed into a house on Cottage street. one night. Luckily for the pilot, one wing hit a tree and the other hit the house, dropping the plane gently to the ground and leaving him unscathed. This 30 days in Gt. Barrington was a wonderful experince with the family and new friends that I met. After my leave ended, I reported to a receiving station in Boston to await further assignment. Three weeks later I was sent to Camp Perry near Williamsburg, Virginia on the James River for advanced base training. There I learned to operate different types of vehicles and machinery: army trucks in convoy, fork lift trucks in the warehouse, motor launches in the river, and cranes for loading and unloading ships. A surprise came when at the end of training, instead of being shipped to bases overseas, I was placed aboard an all purpose destroyer (APD) as a passenger for San Pedro, California to be assigned to the crew of LST 611.

Near the end of July, while still in Virginia, a letter had come from home informing me that Mother had given birth to a son, Charles Edward, on the 26th of July, her 43rd birthday. This was 14 years after the twins, Jerry and Marie, and raised the total to seven children.

As we were cruising down the Atlantic headed for the Panama Canal, the announcement came over the air that the Japanese had surrendered. Celebration broke out and everyone rejoiced that we wouild not be cannon fodder nor victims of Kami-Kazi attacts, and counted their points trying to determine their nearness to discharge rank. It was on this trip that I wrote my third poem.

                          The War is Over
        While cruising down the Atlantic on an APD, newly commissioned and fitted for sea,
        Suddenly there came out of the clear blue sky, the announcement that the japs no longer wished to die.
        They were ready and willing to lay down their arms if their precious little Emperor should suffer no harm.
        The men of the Ray K. Edwards shouted with glee.
        They sang and they danced and had quite a spree.
        Some counted their points to total forty four
        Others looked on and wished for more.
        But they all knew it wouldn't be long
        Before they joined the civilian throng.

The APD stopped at the Panama Canal Zone for a few hours and we were given the opportunity to go ashore for relaxation. before continuing the trip to San Pedro.

The LST to which I was assigned had been towed back to the states after a bomb went through the engine room and was in dry docks for repairs when I arrived. A two week dry run followed repairs and I was assigned to the four man crew of a 40 millimeter anti-aircraft gun for practice sessions with a target towed by aircraft. My job was to take the rack of shells from around the revolving turret and shove them into the top of the gun as it was being aimed and fired. I also was the ship's cook. The LST subsequently left for Pearl Harbor, eventually to go out to the Pacific Islands for salvage work following atom bomb testing. We spent three months at the naval base and had frequent liberty to explore the area. Finally acquiring enough points for discharge, I was transferred to a patrol gunboat headed for the states. (Hawaii was still a territory, not acquiring statehood until 1959).

Considering the reckless endangerment that occured for several years regarding exposure to atomic radiation, I was indeed lucky not to be going out for salvage work

The patrol gunboat, PG 129, was the smallest vessel I had ever been on over the high seas and did considerable weaving and tossing in the heavy waves. For the first and only time in my naval career I got seasick and spent three miserable days before becoming acclimated to the motion. After landing at Treasure Island, I was sent home for a 20 day leave before reporting to Boston for an honorable discharge.

For the last six months of duty, I drew no pay. Making loans to other sailors, poker losers, I would stand near the pay line to collect from them each month, and let my pay ride for an additional nest egg. In addition to the federal mustering out check, a $300 one was received from the state of Massachusetts and later deposited in an account at Tuskegee for emergencies. I had purchased some war bonds through the payroll deduction plan and had them sent home for safekeeping. It was considerably upsetting to discover that my father had cashed them in. When asked why he had done such a thing, he replied, "Well, they said Isaac Crawford. That's my name." From that time on I made sure that all my financial records and accounts were under the name, Isaac Crawford, Jr. The Junior part had been dropped when entering college and the Navy because I was sick of always being addressed as "Junior" by family members.

With six weeks to go before enrolling for the Summer session at Tuskegee, I joined the 52-20 club. This was a program in which the government paid unemployed veterans $20 for 52 weeks. They had to be seeking and available for work through the local unemployment office. Just when I was about to leave for school, a letter came informing me that a job was available with the construction crew for the highway department.

Mother had read that Harvard University was offering scholorships to Blacks to enroll in the school of medicine, and tried to get me interested in that field. Though I enjoyed the sciences such as anatomy, biology and medical technology, the thought of working with sick people did not appeal to me. Also, at almost 22 years of age and having already spent 5 years working and studing in the culinary field, I knew that jobs would always be available, and had no desire to start from scratch in a new field. So I resumed my studies at Tuskegee, completing the last quarter of my sophomore year and beginning as a junior in the Fall. With the G.I. Bill for veterans and a monthly income, alll the required books could be procured, and I made the Dean's list for the last two years. and was able to participate in many social activities.

During my final navy leave I had attended a dance in Pittsfield with my sister, Marie, and had met a young lady named Rosemary Persip whose family was one of the oldest in the Berkshires, tracing their ancestry back to about the time of the Revolutionary War. Sitting beside my sister across the room she asked her, "Who is that guy?" and Marie replied, "Oh, that's just my brother." Although reportedly a former girl friend of Peter who was away in the Army, we shared a few dances and this mutual attraction blossomed into romance. She was a Junior in high school at that time and asked me to accompany her to the Junior-Senior Prom which I gladly accepted. That winter my internship was at O'Brien's Restaurant on a mountain side in Waverly, New York. I managed to come home during one weekend off and spent most of that time at Rosemary's house. It was necessary to fly back and take a taxi in order to get to work on Monday afternoon.

A student in the nursing program at Tuskegee had begun her training at the beginning of my Sophomore year, which meant that we would have graduated together since nursing was a three year program. We had gone to a few movies and dances and were getting pretty close when I was drafted. As often been said, "absence makes the heart grow fonder." We corresponded for three years and became engaged. I sent her an engagement ring purchased with poker winnings while in Hawaii. But upon returning to school, Marjorie Kurtz from Albion Michigan, and I shared a few details of the intervening years and after several long discussions both realized that we had moved on with our lives in different directions and had developed other interests and romances. We mutually agreed to terminate the relationship. I did not ask for, nor receive the ring back.

During the Summer of 1947, I secured an internship as Chef at the Pittsfield Country Club in Pittsfield and Rosemary and I made plans to be married on August 24, 1947 at the First Baptist Church in Pittsfield. Dressed in black tie and tails, the mid 90's temperature of that day was stiffling and to this day maintains the record. A reception was held in the back yard of her parents and catered by her uncle, John Persip, who had a thriving business in that field. Three days off from work had been arranged, railroad tickets purchased, and reservations made at the Lincoln Hotel in New York City for our honeymoon, Some so called friends of hers tried to sabotage our departure and prevented us from getting to the railroad station until after the train had departed. A neighbor of the Persips on Summit Avenue drove us rapidly to Lenox where we missed it again. After rushing to Lee we were finally able to board for the four to five hour trip. Additional excitement was provided the next afternoon when during a brief thunderstorm lightening struck the hotel.

Rosemary and a close friend and classmate, Elizabeth Caesar, Tubby, to her friends, had been accepted as the first blacks into the Nursing program at St. Lukes Hospital in Pittsfield. Elizabeth entered that Fall, but Rosemary's decision to get married ended that option for her as the

Nuns did not take married women into the program at that time. (A topic she frequently raised in later years when things did not go the way she desired.)

Not wishing to subject her to segregation and discrimination of the South immediately, I arranged for us to fly down on returning to Tuskegee in the Fall. We rented a room from a lady who had known the Crawfords when we lived in the community, and stayed there until an apartment became available in the Veterans housing project. just off campus. Rosemary became friends with a neighbor's teen aged daughter and they frequently went shopping in the town of Tuskegee. She was surprised and shocked to discover that white customers were waited on first even though she was first in line, and that she could not use certain bathrooms or drink from certain water fountains labeled "White Only".

The increased allowance for married veterans was fouled up in red tape and did not come through until near the end of the school year, so we had to use some of the emergency fund as well as some of the silver dollars received as a wedding present. We would take the silver to the local grocery store for the end of month purchases and ask the owner to hold them until my check came, at which time we would redeem them during the Winter two instructors and four of us students participated in a hotel-restaurant show at the Civic Center in Miami, Florida where we put on a buffet dinner sponsored by a beer company for participants in the show. Our picture was taken, and later displayed on the cover of a magazine, depicting us demonstrating usage of a radar oven, forerunner to the microwave oven of today. Another highlight of that winter was Rosemary's pregancy which commenced in January of 1948.

Since I had four years of eligibility under the G.I. Bill for education, but only needed a little over two years to complete my studies at Tuskegee, I took flight training as an elective in the Spring quarter at Moton Field. This was the same airport where the Tuskegee Airmen had begun their training and Captain Anderson, who had flown Mrs. Eleanor Roosevelt around the area and had been involved in the early training of the airmen, was also one of my instructors. The other one was Lt. Henderson who took me up for my first orientation flight. and, perhaps wanting to test my mettle, took the unusual step of going into a spin. He was shocked when I started laughing, and thinking I was getting hysterical, asked in alarm, "What's the matter?" "it tickles", I replied. So I flew Piper Cub, Aeronca and Taylor Craft planes for the 25 hours dual and 20 solo to complete training, took a test in meteorology and navigation and received my private pilot's license. The ground instructor came to my apartment to tell me that I had scored 100 % in meteorology. I especially enjoyed the stalls and spins and would often fly over the apartment complex where we lived and do stunts while Rosemary watched and waved from the ground. She would never accompany me on any flight over the years claiming that she doesn't trust me not to do acrobatics while she is aboard. She also has fear of heights and flying and even in commercial flights wants to sit on the aisle seat and not near the window. one day I was asked by one of the instructors to accompany him to a farm field in Georgia where a plane had landed and to fly the plane back to Moton Field. When we approached the farm field he went into a spin until we lost the height and then glided to a landing. Impressed, I decided to do the same landing when I got back to the airport, hoping to impress the staff. Instead I was chewed out for performing such a stunt over a field where planes were taking off and landing.

I had one more internship to do before graduating and did not wish to go all the way back to Tuskegee to pick up my BS degree at the end of the Summer. So before returning as Chef at the Country Club of Pittsfield, arrangements were made for my degree to be mailed to me.

A couple of golfers at the club were students at Williams College and said their fraternity, Phi Delta Theta, was looking for a chef for the coming year. There was also an offer from the Crane Inn In Dalton. Both jobs offered the same amount of money, but the fraternity provided free room and board, so I took that one. We had two rooms and a bath on the lower level near the kitchen. The dining room was upstairs and a dumbwaiter was used to transfer the food for family style service. Working at Williams College provided the opportunity to dramatically increase my proficiency as a chef. I was free to experiment and try a wide variety of recipes and dishes. The only stipulation was that evening meals would have no casseroles as the main course, but chops, steaks, poultry, roasts fish, etc. Rosemary worked in the kitchen as my assistant and began to develop her decorative skills with cakes and icings.

I purchased my first car, a 1941 Ford with 90,000 miles on it and kept it for two and a half years, making numerous repairs until it finally blew a cylinder when returning from a trip to Connecticut. This made me resolve to purchase new cars in the future, low priced economy ones, and to get as much mileage out of them as possible.

31 Summit Avenue, Pittsfield, was the home of Rosemary's parents, Alfred and Augusta Persip. and was used as our mailing address because we spent school vacations in Pittsfield and were employed elsewhere during the Summer. Alfred was a landscape gardener and almost every

conversation would get around to flowers, his pet obsession. He and his brother Charles had served in the Army during World War 1 and were very active in the local American Legion Post, each serving a term as president. Charles was Sargeant at Arms for about fifty years and when he died, the post was renamed in his honor. They both gave me a gift of membership, and in their memory, I retain my membership to this day, although I don't participate in many Legion events.

On October 27, 1948 Rosemary visited her obstetrician, Dr. Daniel Dorman, in Pittsfield for a routine check-up. He said everything was fine and he would see her again in two weeks. that night around midnight, she woke me with the news that her water had broken and she was going into labor. Hurridly dressing and rushing to Pittsfield, we drove to her Mother's house and called Dr. Dorman. He suggested coming immediately to St. Lukes Hospital where he would meet her. About an hour later, around 2 a.m. Rosemary, Jr. made her appearance.

Most of the students in the late forties and early fifties were graduates of private prep schools and sons of wealthy corporate executives or professionals. The college was not coed at that time except during house party weekends when dates arrived from many of the prestigious girl's schools. By the mid fifties, the college sought to change its image and to recruit more public school students from lower income families. As a consequence, the schism that this created socially was obvious, and indicated that the days of exclusive fraternities would soon be over. Considering myself the intellectual equal of these younger fellows, I was always willing to debate any issue and had some lively discussions with Kevin White, the house president who later became mayor of Boston. Kevin had stomach ulcers, and in the suggested high fat treatment of that time period, frequently came to the kitchen for scrambled eggs or cream rich milk. In a discussion of race, Kevin said he had no prejudices, but there had been one black in his prep school class who was an uppity S.0.B. I pointed out that probably all of his previous contacts with blacks had been with servants who maintained an air of docility and subservience in order to maintain their job, and he found it difficult to accept a minority member on an equal footing who had a similar background and education to his. The debate became more heated when Kevin saw a picture in the paper of a black coed at an Illinois college who had been crowned home-coming queen, and remarked that he wouldn't mind dating her. I was reminded of the time when my family lived in the community off campus at Tuskegee. I was out in the yard in front of the house when three white youths in a car pulled up and one of them asked, Y'all got any sisters?" Surmising their intentions, I said "No", and they drove on.

As the end of the 1949 school year approached, I responded to an ad in a New York paper and received the job as chef at a children's camp, Camp Wi-Co-Suto, on Newfound Lake between Bristol and Plymouth, New Hampshire, and took along as my crew, my wife, her sister, Eleanor, and my brother, Jerry. The next two summers were spent at Camp Mohawk on Cheshire Lake in Cheshire Massachusetts. In 1952, I switched to resorts and worked as chef at Seven Hills in Lenox. The following summer, 1953, was spent at the Oakwood Inn in Great Barrington with Rosemary as my assistant. Here again, lightening came close. During an afternoon thunderstorm, there was a sudden flash outside and a big ball of flame leaped out of the light fixture overhead.

At the end of the summer of 1953, Rosemary announced that she had had enough of cooking and wanted to explore other avenues. I didn't realize at the time that this also applied to her husband) She and young Rosemary remained in Pittsfield at her parent's house and she began working as a nurse's aide at St. Lukes Hospital. I came down from Williamstown every weekend and some nights during the week. A few thousand dollars had been saved up during the first five years completed at Williams College, so a search was begun for a house in the Pittsfield area. By December a decision had been made to purchase a two bedroom house at 41 Lakeway Drive in Pittsfield from a GE transferee who was moving South. The price was $13,500. A G.I. mortgage at 4-1/2 % was secured at the Union Federal Savings and Loan Bank. I then commuted daily to Williamstown for the next four years. I returned to the Oakwood Inn in the summer of 1954, and then went to the Music Inn in Lenox for the last three years of my available summers, 1955 through 1957. Music Inn, like many of the former millionaire's estates in Lenox had been converted to an Inn for summer tourists. Located on the east side of Stockbridge Bowl, the property had several buildings that were converted to unique usages. The carriage house became the main Inn with kitchen and dining facilities. The ice house was used as as dwelling place for the owners, Philip and Stephanie Barbour. The horse barn and stalls became the site for jazz concerts on the lower level and rooms on the upper levels. a greenhouse became a night time cafe for drinks and dancing. The jazz concerts featured some of the musical giants of that era: The Modern Jazz Quartet, Dave Bruebeck Quartet, Duke Ellington, Count Basie, Dizzy Gillespie, The Dorsey Brothers, Sarah Vaughn, Jerry Mulligan, Billy Taylor and Ethyl Waters to name a few. Employees and their families could attend the concerts for free, so we spent many nights listening to great jazz.

Rosemary suffered a miscarriage in 1955, but became pregnant again the following year. She had been fitted with a diaphram to prevent pregnancy after Rosmary's birth. We had to go to Albany, New York for the procedure as the Blue Laws of Massachusetts did not permit doctors to do anything to prevent conception or childbirth. After several years, and especially after her miscarriage, another child was desired. On September 20, 1956, she gave birth to a son, Isaac Allen, at St. Lukes Hospital in Pittsfield.

The fraternity house in Williamstown did not agree with my request for a salary increase so I ended my nine years there in June, 1957. At the completion of the summer at Music Inn, I decided to try the glamorous life of a salesperson and became a salesman for Electrolux vacuum cleaners. There was no salary. Income was based on a generous percentage of each sales contract. Unfortunately, that was a time of layoffs for GE, and many of the unemployed sought refuge in selling vacuum cleaners also. No territory was assigned. Everyone was free to cover any section of the county so desired. It was not unusual to go out in the boondocks expecting to make a killing and have some irate homeowners greet you with, "What are you guys pulling"? There have been a half dozen people here already this week with the same spiel". The first week or so was fine. But after making sales to relatives and acquaintances, the bottom fell out and I realized that it was time to resume looking for a job in my field.

In November, I began the first of my ten year full time employment as Chef at the Log Cabin restaurant in Lenox. This was a gourmet restaurant with about 18 regular entree items, except for a few seasonal changes, A high fat and high cholesterol diet was an acceptable practice in those days and the two biggest sellers on the menu were Roast Prime Rib of Beef Au Jus and Broiled Sirloin Steak. A thick slice of beef was served and the regular steaks were 16 ounces. An extra one weighing 20 ounces could be ordered. Other popular items included Broiled Lobster, Fried Shrimp and Fried or Baked Scallops. Winter nights were often slow, with heavy snow and zero temperatures; but during the weekends of Tanglewood three and four hundred dinners would be served from 5 p.m. until well past midnight. all entrees except Roast Beef were cooked to order and accompanied by a choice of potatoes, vegetables and salad. In the heat of that small basement kitchen with its low ceiling and hot broiler, grill, fryers, ovens and stovetop, I would frequently go home 7 pounds lighter than when I went to work—mostly through dehydration despite drinking gallons of fluid all night.

With prep schools nearby, along with the Berkshire Playhouse, Tanglewood, Music Inn, and Jacob's Pillar, many celebrities were dinner guest: Harry Belafonte, Jackie Robinson, Dinah Washington, Eddie

Fisher, Ann Bancroft, Dana Andrews, Arthur Fiedler, Sergi Ozawa, plus many others. Belafonte and Robinson had offspring who attended prep schools in the nearby community. One Sunday afternoon, Lennie Wolf, oo-owner and manager of the restaurant came down to the kitchen and said, "Come upstairs with me. I want you to meet someone." As we entered the dining room, I recognized Jackie Robinson standing at the bar. The wary expression on his face gave clear evidence that he did not relish this encounter and probably thought it was an attempt on the management's part to humilate him. When introduced, he stuck out his hand, said, "Hi", and immediately turned his back. Returning to the kitchen, I felt sorry for him that he could not rise above the situation and show a little common courtesy. I also remembered the words of my Sociology professor in college when Jackie broke into the major leagues and was touted as a credit to his race and doing it for their benefit. My professor said to the class. "He is not doing it for me, He's doing it for Jackie Robinson."

After a few more years of the same basic menu in a poor working environment, in spite of promises to construct a new facility, I began to explore other opportunities and responded to several advertised openings. Desiring more of a mental challenge, I submitted my resume as part of an application for a food service director's job at Yale University and was informed that I had just the qualifications they were looking for, and to come down for a lunch and interview. But when I walked in the door and gave my name, the administrator was suddenly too busy to meet with me. An underling was assigned to show me around and take me to lunch in the cafeteria. A few weeks later I received a letter saying the position had been filled. I also applied for a position with General Electric in Pittsfield and received a very favorable recommendation from their personnel director who interviewed me. Taken to lunch and shown around the facilities by management, I was offered two openings; Time and Motion Studies, or Stock Room Inventories. Neither appealed to me as I was most interested in Public Relations. Luckily I did not accept employment at GE because a few years later they started downsizing their facilities and transferring or eliminating employees prior to closing the Pittsfield location. As a new employee I would have been one of the first to go and would not have accumulated any benefits. So I decided to remain at the Log Cabin while I went to graduate school and into education.

Because of increasing marital problems, I had filed for a divorce and put the house up for sale. Counseling had been recommended but had no positive results because of denials and coverups. The house was sold at a loss of $5,000 because I had overimproved it for the neighborhood., and with the cut back in GE operations, the prices of homes had dropped. But, in spite of the obstacles, It was decided to continue the marriage.

We moved into a two bedroom apartment in Colonial Gardens near the Dalton town line with the exception of Rosemary, Jr. who elected to be on her own and shared an apartment with a girl friend in Pittsfield. She had finished high school, attended Berkshire Community College and been employed at a bank and at Berkshire Life Insurance Company as a secretary. Our son, Isaac Allen, was a fifth grade student at Bartlett Elementary school on Onota Street near Lakeway Drive, and transfered to Allendale in the new neighborhood. He later went to Nessacus in Dalton in the sixth grade and became active in Junior football and the Boy Scouts.

In the Summer of 1966 I enrolled in The graduate program at North Adams State College and began taking courses for a Masters degree in Education during the morning and working afternoons and evenings at the restaurant. In the Fall I took two night courses and worked the other five. I also substituted several times in the science department at Wahconah Regional High School in Dalton. I applied for an opening at Cheshire Elementary School to begin in 1967 and was hired to teach fifth and sixth grade Geography and sixth grade English. Because of the low starting salary for teachers at that time period, I worked Friday, Saturday and Sunday nights in the restaurant, often correcting papers between orders during the slower seasons of Fall and Winter.

A very interesting relationship developed with my sixth grade home room class at Cheshire. In English class we were discussing poetry and I began to recite a poem I had memorized half of while in elementary school; "The Ride of Jenny McNeal". when I got to The part that said: "Hark! From the hills a moment mute, came the clatter of hoofs in hot pursuit. And a cry from the foremost trooper said, Halt, or your blood be on your head. She heeded it not and not in vain. She lashed the horse with the bridal rein. The raindrops gasped at her glowing face. The pebbles flew from the fearful race. Hark, once more came the voice of dread. Halt, or your blood be on your head." I stopped and told the excited class that that was as far as I could go. They were very disappointed and eager to hear the outcome. So I assured them that I would go to the Pittsfield library and get a copy to share with them.

I only had a problem with one professor in the graduate program at North Adams State College. He was an instructor at Williams College and was moonlighting for evening courses in Philosophy. He frequently arrived about ten minutes late for class dressed in his sports outfit as a tennis player. On this particular night he came in and told the class to write for a half hour about the life of Socrates. I sat there meditating for a while and summarized my thoughts. When I received the response, he had written, "This is great. But it is only a beginning. You were supposed to write for a half hour."; I told him that was my style; to give serious thought to a topic and then to write a summary. He gave me a C for that semester and the one that followed. Since graduate students with more than two C's were not allowed to complete the program, I made sure that I went overboard in my work and finished the last six classes with straight A's.

Rosemary had switched from being a nurse's aid to taking the Operating Room Technician Course at St Lukes Hospital which she completed and began to work in Surgery.

An opening as a Chef Instructor was available at McCann Technical School in North Adams for the Culinary program. I applied and was accepted. Receiving my Masters Degree in June of 1968, I began at Mcann Tech in September, teaching six classes per day in related theory: math, nutrition, food preparation, menu planning, baking and food cost control.

I received a brochure from the Council on hotel, restaurant and Institutional Education (CHRIE) inviting me to register for their three day conference in New Orleans over the Christmas recess. The school agreed to pay my expenses and I flew down for for the first of 18 such conferences I would attend over my 21 years at McCann. The schedule was subsequently moved to the Summer months and was frequently used as a family vacation in many major cities in the USA and in Canada. I returned with many enthusiastic ideas and drafted an eight page typewritten report for the superintendent—director, Jim Westall. He was impressed and said he was thinking of making some of the very same changes I suggested. The School Lunch Director was leaving at the end of the school year and Mr. Westall asked if I would like to combine the two jobs as director of Culinary Arts and director of School Food Services. Students in the program would prepare the school breakfast and lunch meals for half of the school year and the other half would be spent in the school restaurant kitchen, dining room and bake shop. Freshmen and Juniors were in one group and Sophomores and Seniors in the other. Qualified Juniors and Seniors could also be assigned to Co—op interrnships in Restaurants. This job involved a substantial increase in pay and the work was challenging and rewarding even though it called for about 10 hours per day at school plus a couple of hours at home. My time was divided between the classroom, two offices, and out on the floor getting involved in and supervising food preparation. Then after school or at night at home, there was class preparation, papers to correct, menu planning for the breakfast and lunch program, etc. I was definitely no longer bored.

Our daughter eloped to New York State with Charles Wilder, a boy she had been dating against her parents wishes. We found out the hard way that expressing disapproval is the quickest way to unite a couple. Charles had no money, no trade or profession, and little fondness for work. In December of 1968 she gave birth to a son, Eric. born three months premature and the second smallest child to survive at Berkshire Medical Center at that time. It was four months before he could go home. After three years of discord, the marriage ended in divorce. She worked as a school bus driver, a custodian, and later, as a security guard at General Electric in Pittsfield, before deciding to move to California with her son in the late seventies.

At a Christmas party at the home of the school librarian in December of 1968 I became fascinated with her log cabin home and intrigued with the idea of building one as a cheaper alternative to a convential home. All things considered, it was not cheaper, but did afford my son and me the opportunity to do a great deal of the work ourselves. The librarian, Mrs. Jensen, provided me with the name and location of the agent in Mt. Snow, Vermont, who was the sales representative for Pan Abode, the company in Renton, Washington that manufactured the houses made of Western Cedar. Rosemary and I drove up to Vermont and spent hours inspecting the agent's house and going over the options for number of rooms and layout. I ordered the house to be delivered in June of 1969 so that most of the Summer could be used for construction. Isaac Allen and I drove around through several communities looking for an ideal location for such a house and found a one acre lot for sale on Kirchner Road in Dalton. There were several dozen large pine trees across the site and the area near the street was lined with maple trees. A small brook meandered through the rear of the lot and created the idea of someday building a pond. I was shocked when the Dalton Building inspector withheld the permit until I provided detailed information from the company. He claimed he didn't understand what was going to hold the logs together and be used for partitions, etc., even though I said log cabin houses had been around for 200 years and were still in existence. Cedar does not rot. This was to be the second one in Berkshire County and the first one in our area. So I had to withhold payment for the house while the company sent me detailed blueprint plans and layouts for the inspector. Finally receiving approval, Delivery was scheduled for August. Meanwhile, trees had been cut down, stumps removed, grading and excavation completed, the foundation poured and the deck put on. When the freight car arrived with its cargo of lincoln logs, I picked up a bunch of teen aged boys to help unload in the alloted two days and rented a truck for transport. With one hired retired carpenter and ocassional assistance from family and friends, we put the six room house together in three weeks. It took an eight pound sledge hammer and a batter board to lock the logs together and I ended up with Carpal Tunnel Syndrome of both wrists which later required surgery to correct. The finished work took considerably longer. I subcontracted the plumbing and heating, electrical installation, wall to wall carpeting and a field stone fireplace. Luckily, an addition was being built at McCann Tech and was behind schedule, so the students didn't start until October. Teachers put in a few hours each morning and then went home. I was frequently pounding roofing nails by moonlight. By the end of November we moved in and celebrated Thanksgiving in our new home. The satisfaction of completing a do-it-yourself project, plus the opportunity to bond with my son and discuss many topics and issues as he approached puberty, were beyond measure. Three years later, A reporter from the Berkshire Eagle scheduled an appointment to come out and interview us about the house and take a few pictures of the place which is included.

In addition to the Chrie Conferences, I continued to take courses for professional improvement at North Adams and Westfield State Colleges and became certified in Special Education and Teaching with Computers. Chrie was an international organization for educators in the hospitality field and I served as a high school and technical school representative on the board of directors and as treasurer of the organization for a two year period. I was nominated for president one year but lost out on a close vote. In 1985, I received the Achievement Award at the conference in Seattle, Washington for having started a fund raising gourmet dinner at McCann Tech in 1984 for the purpose of providing scholarships in the culinary field for Seniors who had the ability and desire to continue their education. We also took them on field trips to culinary schools and to dinner in a first class restaurant. That practice has continued since my retirement thanks to one of my former students, Pat Cariddi, who was given my job after my recommendation. A reporter for the Berkshire Eagle had written a full page article about the dinner following an interview with me and included the menu, recipes, my resume and picture.

At McCann Tech, I served as vice president and president of the faculty association and later as chairman of the contract negotiations committee.

I was asked to join the Board of the North Berkshire Conference of Christians and Jews even though I did not live in that area, and eventually served terms as vice president and president of that organization. Each year a person was selected from one of the North Berkshire communities to receive an award for outstanding and dedicated community service to others at an awards dinner.

About a dozen professional Blacks in Pittsfield started an investment group called Partners in Progress, with the intention of building a financial base for our retirement years. We bought several apartment houses at foreclosure sales and through sweat equity restored them to code specifications. They were then rented to low income families at a reasonable rate. Our goal was two fold. Sure we wanted to make a small profit; but we additionally wanted to assist our poorer neighbors, who in general, were relegated to certain sections of town. To our utter dismay, we had several families who paid the security deposit and one month's rent, and then never paid another cent. Evictions sometimes took six months or longer thanks to a district court judge who had no regard for our plight, and once had us pay to move a family out. One couple, when finally made to move, took a broom handle and jabbed holes in the shreetrock walls and smeared feces over the walls. One building we were trying to sell was unoccupied for a few months and was dropped from the insurance list. Naturally, it was set on fire and we lost our shirts. The only redeeming factor was that our loses could be written off for tax purposes over a period of years.

General Electric had a number of Blacks in management and sales in response to the government's demand that firms dealing with federal contracts had to demonstrate equal opportunity employment. This small nuceleus started an organization called The Minority Council on Community Concerns and got other Blacks in the area to join. The main purpose was to provide scholarships for minorities furthering their education. Solicitations from industries and an annual cocktail party provided the major source of funds and thousands of dollars were awarded to academically successful minority students, I served as treasurer and also a term as president. In a few years, as part of it's planned exodus from Pittsfield, the majority of Blacks were transferred or terminated by GE, and the Minority council turned over its assets to the Second Congregational Church, a Black church which had a scholarship program of its own.

In the late sixties, Mayor Remo Del Gallo in response to a request from the Pittsfield area Council of churches, appointed me to the Code

Enforcement Commission. One reporter labeled me as the lonesomest man in town because all of the other members of the commission were city officials. I was supposedly the neighborhood representative.

Although I had attended First Baptist Church off and on since Rosemary and I were married there in 1947, I did not become an official member until 1954. The Reverend Christian Jensen got me involved in a number of church activities and I served on the Social Action Committee and the Diaconate. Under subsequent minnisters, I served on the Board of Trustees, Nominating Committee, Music Committee and as a Sunday School teacher and choir member. Most of these latter activities began when I left the restaurant and went into teaching, which gave me Sunday mornings and evenings off. I also joined the Berkshire Lyric Theater chorus a few years later and participated in a number of Musical plays; (Most Happy Fella, Dido and Annaeus, Student Prince and The Magic Chord) thanks to our choir director, Terry Forrest, who sang in that group and taught music at Taconic High School. I had always enjoyed singing even though I couldn't read music at that time. I would listen to Billy Eckstein, Mario Lanza, Bing Crosby, Nat King Cole, etc. and sing whatever song they sang in the same way. At that time I had a three octive range and could sing whatever I heard. I enrolled in a home study course to learn to read music and to play the piano. Unfortunately, I could not look at the notes and words and the keys at the same time and stay in tempo. So I bought a chord organ and a keyboard and only had to use a couple of fingers and eventually knew where the appropiate keys were located and could follow the music. I was also doing solos in Church over the years and still do at the present time. I was asked to do a speech on Brotherhood Sunday at the North Adams First Baptist Church and there was an article in the North Adams transcript about it.

Isaac Allen graduated from Wahconah Regional H.S. in 1974 and enrolled at American Internationl College in Springfield, MA, majoring in Business Administration. He had worked with me a few times in the restaurant and had helped out on catering jobs, so I suggested Hotel/Restaurant Administration. He didn't seem too interested so the matter was dropped. I had sense enough to realize that parents should not try to push their kids into any field that was not high on the offspring's priority list. He went out for football and ended up as a sub without too much playing time. Isaac A. was active in student government and minority groups and in the theater, starring in a musical play. He also did some duets with me over the years at church and one Sunday, My wife and daughter joined us for a quartet.

Receiving his B.A. degree in 1978, he worked for two years as an insurance adjustor for Travelers Insurance in their Worcester office, followed by two years as a personnel recruiter for Stone and Webster in their Boston office. He then secured a job as a Personnel recruiter for a Black owned computer firm, Input-Output Computer Service (IOCS), and swiftly rose to a vice presidency of sales and marketing. While in Springfield He had met a young lady named Gwendolyn Gasque, who was a graduate of Wilberforce University and was employed by Mass Mutual Insurance. She was five years older than he, but the mutual attraction led to a courtship and an engagement. She went to work for Digital Computers and swiftly rose to one of the chief financial positions. A large wedding was planned for them on June 26, 1982 in her home town in South Carolina with about 25 people in the bridal party. and three ministers: ours from First Baptist, Dale Lock; Gwen's from a church in Springfield; and the minister of the church in South Carolina. After a honeymoon in Bermuda, they rented an apartment in Nashua, New Hampshire for a while before purchasing their first home. A daughter, Jillion Ashley, was born on January 24, 1987, with a cleft lip which was corrected by surgery a few months later.

In California, Rosemary, Jr. met a fellow, Vernell smith, on a tour bus for Las Vegas and the ensuing romance led her to contemplate marriage once again. They came home for a big wedding at First Baptist Church in Pittsfield; something she had missed with her earlier elopement. My wife made the wedding gown and some of the gowns for the bridesmaids. She also made and decorated the wedding cake. We rented a large tent and had it set up on the front lawn for the reception. I prepared most of the food in advance but hired a young chef to supervise the set-up and service. After the celebration, Rosemary and Vernell and her son, Eric Wilder, returned to Los Angeles. In 1983, her brother Isaac, convinced her to move to Nashua. They packed their furniture and other belongings in a huge rented trailer and set out cross crountry. The heavily loaded truck tourned out to be a gas guzzler and by the time they got to Pennsylvania their money had run out. I received a call to drive to their location, pay for a fill-up, and accompany them home.

Rosemary worked for Wang in Lowell and Vernell got a job with Isaac's firm, IOCS, headquartered in Waltham, MA. Two children were born to this union: Richard Isaac in May, 1984 and Vanessa Renee in November, 1985.

I had resumed flying in 1978 by getting checked out in a Cessna 52 and 172, and joining the fifteen member South Mountain Flying Club who collectively owned a 172. So when Richard was born and scheduled to come home from the hospital, I decided to fly up to Nashua for the weekend and see my latest grandchild. A weather check with flight service revealed marginal conditions and the recommendation that the flight not be made since I was not instrument rated and had to fly under visual flight rules (VFR) which required three miles of visibility. My heart was set on going especially since it was sunny in the Berkshires. Following my heart and not my head, I took off and everything was fine until I approached the Connecticut River valley and saw a wall of drizzle and low clouds coming towards me. I had to drop below the correct altitude and manuever between the hills to maintain my orientation. When I was near New Hampshire fog started rolling in and panic began to set in. Visions of having to land in a pasture or on a highway danced in my head. Suddenly, out of the fog, I saw a large runway in front of me and immediately prepared to land without any contact with the tower for permission. There were pot holes and wooden horses positioned along the runway which was under repair. As I manuevered to a safe stop lights were turned on me and a truck came out to escort me to authorities who chewed me out for not contacting them. They directed me to the Nashua airport which was only a few miles away. I had landed in Manchester. They also reported me to the FAA who later sent me a letter ordering me to fly to Westfield for a pilotage flight with an FAA official. He had me plot a flight to a small airport about 30 miles away, and when I approached the field he said to turn around and go home. I had passed the test.

It rained heavily all day Saturday and Sunday morning and it wasn't until late Sunday afternoon that I could safely leave Nashua and fly back to Pittsfield. after visiting with my grandson and his family. The very unpredictable weather in this area was the main reason why I did not schedule any long flights and mostly flew for practice and sight seeing and videos in the Berkshires and neighboring states.

Gwen received a promotion and a transfer to the Digital office in the San Jose area in 1989. Snce she held a much higher position, Isaac A. decided to leave his job and seek employment in San Jose. But his boss said that he had been considering opening a western office for their firm and offered Isaac the opportunity to start the venture. The future looked rosy. They bought a home in surburbia. Isaac soon had three offices going: one each in San Jose, Seattle and Los Angeles. Jillion began attending a private school for the gifted. Then the bottom fell out of the computer industry. Gwen was laid off and didn't find a comparable position for nine months. IOCS decided in 1993 to close the western offices and concentrate on the East coast only. Not wishing to come back to New England, Isaac started doing consulting work and making plans to start his own business, While making huge incomes they had both become accustomed to living high on the hog and spending every penny. With a large mortgage and expensive cars to pay for and maintain, they had to file for bankruptcy. My efforts over the years to teach fiscal planning and responsibility had fallen on deaf ears as Isaac tried to match his wife in spending.

Martha Jane Wright Crawford, Matriarch of the family, died at Springside Nursing Home Pittsfield on April 4, 1989 at the age of 86, a little over three months before her 87th birthday. She had been in declining health for several years and when placed in a nursing home in March, decided it was time to go to her heavenly reward. She had resided with Ruth and her husband, Thomas Evans, in Pittsfield from shortly after Isaac, Sr's. death in 1978.

The house in Great Barrington had been sold and Mother wanted to divide the proceeds among her six living children and Pearl's three kids. I, as administrator convinced her that that money might be needed in later years to provide for her care; and if that contingency occured, probably not all siblings would cough up an equal share. So the funds were placed in certificates of deposit and money market accounts. A few thousand dollars was spent to add a first floor bathroom for her convenience at Ruth's home and a large tombstone was purchased for the burial site of Isaac, Sr., next to whom she would eventually be placed. Interest rates started a spectacular climb over the next few years leading to a doubling of the initial investment. Upon her demise, as per her wishes, when the deposits matured the family was assembled and the remainder was divided into seven equal shares ; one each for each of the six children and one share to be divided three ways for Pearl's offspring.

It was shortly after Mother's death that I wrote the following article.

Parental Farewell

Showing emotions, outside of anger, was never a strong point in our family. I can't remember ever being hugged or kissed as a child by my parents. A handshake was the usual hello and goodbye of our meetings. Perhaps I am partly to blame. Having been on my own since shortly before my 17th birthday and having to survive in a hostile world, I had to learn to control my true feelings.

When I visited Great Barrington, conversations with Daddy were usually limited to sports, hunting and politics. Mother and I discussed a wide variety of family issues, conditions and religious topics. She often provided tickets for dinners or concerts as fund raisers for Macedonia Baptist Church.

When daddy was in the Veterans Hospital in Boston for almost a month recuperating from a bout of Pneumonia as a result of sitting in a cold car for three hours during the blizzard of 78, a young resident physician took away his medication for his heart that he had been taking since 1970 as a result of a minor heart attack, telling him; "You don't need that stuff any more". Sitting in a chair by his bed the night before he was scheduled to come home. he suffered a massive stroke and expired. I received the news in a late night phone call. It was the first death in the immediate family in 28 years—since Pearl died in 1950. Finding it impossible to go to sleep with all the thoughts and memories running through my head, I plugged in the earphones on the organ and sat down and played for hours with the tears streaming down my face. I played hymns, especially "Nearer My God To Thee", which was one of daddy's favorites. Perhaps my grief was intensified by the fact that my 53 years up to that point had been devoid of a close father—son relationship. This lack probably also accounted for the extra effort on my part to communicate with my children and be there for them.

When Daddy died, Mother, who had spent so many years catering to his needs, seemed to abdicate responsibility for her own welfare, and ocassionally to lose touch with reality as physical disability and memory loss accelerated. When she could no longer manage on her own. she moved in with Ruth and Tommie Evans for the next ten years and the house in Great Barrington was sold. It was during this period that I was trying to accumulate additional family data and do a profile on all known family members. Mother couldn't remember events she had talked about many years ago and would frequently look to Ruth for answers to questions.

In March of 1989 she spent about a week at Berkshire Medical Center for tests and evaluations. Tommie was dying of cancer at home and Ruth was in no position to take care of two semi invalids. So the decision was made to place Mother in an extended care facility, more commonly referred to as a nursing home. 86 years old, crippled, incontinent and partially blind, she made the decision that it was, in her words, "Time to go". Refusing nourishment she wasted away and was dead in three weeks. She could have been returned to the hospital, placed on machines and force fed to keep her alive for an indefinate period., but the family decided against this tactic, believing that it was better to let her go peacefully to the heavenly reward she so eagerly anticipated and awaited.

A couple of days before the end I went to visit and found her softly and continuously singing hymns of her faith. The nurse said Mother had been doing this for hours. Wouldn't that be harmful, I inquired. "Well, her lungs are in good shape and she's getting exercise", the nurse replied.

The next day, I went by after school and found her rational and quiet. We chatted for a time and I offered her some water which she drank. We held hands and a quiet peace enveloped us as she drifted off to sleep. The next morning the dreaded phone call came. I was glad that a premonition had prompted my last visit with her.

Retirement Years

Teachers in Massachusetts can work until the age of 70, but I chose to retire at 65 in June of 1989. Not expecting a long life, there were other things I wanted to do with my remaining years; some paid, but mostly volunteer activities. The paid ones took place the first couple of years. I did follow up surveys for the 1990 and 2000 Census Bureau during the Summer and early Fall, covering the hill towns around central Berkshire many of which had lakeside vacation homes only used a short period of the year, mostly Summers. I taught two semesters part time of Hotel Restaaurant Management at Berkshire Community College, and thus could could claim to have taught on three levels; elementary, high school and college. I took a night course in woodworking at Taconic high and built a 5 x 8 foot bookcase and a router table and cabinet. Century Cable Television offered free training for volunteers for their South County community channel. I attended about a dozen sessions on camera operation, lighting, directing, programming and editing. In December of 91, I joined the volunteer crew at the recently opened Dalton Community Cable TV channel and soon began producing and editing my own program, "Ike's Forum", and became a member of the board of directors and vice president. After serving several terms on the board of directors of the American Baptist Churches of Massachusetts, TABCOM, I was selected for a two year term, 1991-1992, as president of the organization that included more than 260 Baptist Churches in the state.

Softball and volleyball were dropped from my list of recreational activities after a muscle was pulled in running the bases, but I have continued to be involved in golf and bowling.

I also began to videotape the George Morrell Show in Nursing homes and to sing an uplifting song or hymn as part of the program. Then we taped shows at his house, at the studio, at my house and at a music store.

But after about 15 years, I called it quits.

September 1994 marked the 50th anniversary of the founding of Macedonia Baptist Church in Great Barrington by my parents, especially the work of my Mother, Martha Jane Wright Crawford, who had attended a missionary Bible School in Chicago and spent most of her life engaged in religious activities.

I was invited to speak at a dinner celebration honoring that historic date and gave the following presentation.

Macedonia Baptist Church Celebration
50th Anniversary Dinner September 24,1994

Subject:: **"Moving into the Future With Faith"**

One Evening last month I received a call from Mrs. Forte, Wife of the Minister at Macedonia Baptist Church, the Reverend Joseph Forte, informing me of the 50th anniversary of the Church and that a dinner was to be held on the 24th of September to honor the memory of the founders, Martha and Isaac Crawford, Sr. She asked if I would be one of the speakers on that occasion, and that she would get back to me later with more details. assuming that she merely wanted me to say a few words about the family's involvement with the church, I readily agreed and promptly forgot about the matter.

Last week I came home from choir rehearsal and was handed a telephone message from Mrs. Forte listing a title for a speech and chapter and verse of scripture and asking me to call her the next day. I said to my wife; "That sounds like a sermon." She said; "Well, you're used to standing in front of a group of people." "Yes", I replied, "but as a teacher, master of cermonies or presiding over a board or committee meeting, not to deliver a speech." A call to Mrs Forte revealed that she did indeed want me to be the principal speaker, and her persuasiveness was sufficient to override my feeble protests. So! here I am!

The topic suggested was "Moving into the Future with Faith". The Scripture reading is taken from the Book of Mark, Chapter 11: Verses 22 through 24.

"And Jesus answered them, "Have faith in God. Truly I say to you, whoever says to this mountain, Be taken up and cast into the sea, and does not doubt in his heart, but believes that what he says will come to pass, it will be done for him.

Therefore I tell you, whatever you ask in prayer, believe that you receive it, and you will.

According to the dictionary, faith has several meanings:

1. Belief in God
2. Fidelity to ones promises or allegiance to duty or to a person: loyalty
3. That which is believed, especially a system of religious beliefs.

4. Complete confidence, especially to someone or something open
   to question or suspicion

As professed christians, most of us believe in God as our Father, in Jesus Christ as our Lord and Savior, in the teachings of the Bible, and in the power of prayer. Now that is as it should be and is wonderful, but, I submit, it is not enough. Can we sit back and let the world drift into complete chaos and hope that God will take care of all the problems besetting society?

Daily we are besieged with news of drug abuse, especially crack cocaine, youngsters killing each other over trivia, single mothers at an increasingly younger age, rampant crime, deteriorating schools and educational standards, and less and less respect for parents and teachers or anyone else in authority. This is no longer confined mainly to the inner cities but is spreading rapidly to smaller cities and towns and neighborhoods across the land.

A recent series in the Berkshire Eagle focused on the drug situation in Pittsfield and the brazeness of pushers of crack, many of whom come in from other cities. One article stated that 85 % of drug customers are white. Yet practically all of the stories of pushers and users and neighborhood concerns were about Blacks. Incidently, almost all of the arrests involving possession and distribution were Black. The big dealers remain anonymous and safe. There is a vast backlog of young minorities willing to risk arrest, or even death, for a chance to make big bucks. something no menial job, even if available, would pay.

Now my Mother, Martha Jane Wright Crawford, whom you are honoring tonight, was deeply religious and had great faith. Others will tell you about her missionary zeal and her involvement with the church, but I want to focus on one timeless cliche that we children kept hearing as we were growing up. Whenever we wanted to do something or had goals that seemed beyond achievement, especially those that required financing, her response was always "Where there's a will, there is a way".

Sounds too simplistic and certainly is not the response children wish to hear. In retrospect, however, there has to be a strong desire, an inner drive, an urge to get things done. When I finished High School and wanted to go to college, there was no money available,. so I spent a year at odd jobs; making deliveries on a coal and wood truck, working in a shoe repair shop, and serving as a dishwasher in a restaurant. Then I picked a field, Commercial Dietetics and Food Administration, now called Culinary Arts and Hotel Restaurant Management, a five year program that provided some income through alternate quarters of academics and internships and could be accomplished in 4 years by going year round. I received a total of $2 from home, had no textbooks, a scanty wardrobe, and in the Spring of my Sophomore year was so far behind in my college bills that the treasurer gave me an ultimatum: "Come up with the money or I would have to leave". That same week I received greetings from Uncle Sam, spent three years in the U.S. Navy and as they say, "the rest is history".

After the war the G.I. Bill allowed me to complete college and later go to graduate school and finance a home at a low interest rate.

The point of all this is to differentiate between the "Where there is a will, there is a way" of Martha Crawford and the will and way of much of contemporary society, Mrs. Crawford believed in setting goals and striving to achieve them in spite of often overwhelming obstacles, of having the inner drive, the self motivation, the staying power to see a task through, but always in the framework of consistency with moral, ethical and religious standards.

The current issue of Ebony Magazine features an article about the famed black educator, Dr. Benjamin E. Mayes, the deceased former president of Morehouse College. One of his favorite sayings was "He who starts behind in the race of life must run faster or forever remain behind." He also wrote:

"It must be borne in mind that the tragedy in life doesn't lie in not reaching your goal. The tragedy lies in having no goal to reach. It isn't a calamity to die with dreams unfulfilled, but it is a calamity not to dream. It is not a disaster to be unable to capture your ideal, but it is a disaster to have no ideal to capture. It is not a disgrace not to reach the stars, but it is a disgrace to have no stars to reach for. Not failure but low aim is sin."

Todays youth often want instant success: good grades without study, high income without work, instant gratification of all their desires, children without parental responsibility, and power and dominance by any means. What accounts for this complete reversal?

I say "PARENTS". Childrens lives are shaped and molded from infaancy to young adulthood by the home environment. Poverty is no legitimate excuse.

Few families were poorer than we were on a farm in the backwoods of Alabama for part of our childhood. But we were given chores and responsibility at an early age. We were taught to read and write even before we started to school. We were taken to Sunday School and church services and learned of Jesus and his teachings. We lived by rules of conduct. There were strict guidelines as to what we could and could not do.

The majority of today's marriages end in divorce or separation. many couples live together without benefit of marriage and simply walk away when the going gets tough. Teenage girls are having babies to find the love that was missing in their family or to leave home and go on welfare.

They are incapable of supplying the wholesome nuturing environment essential for successful child rearing. Many couples both work and children are frequently left on their own after school and during vacations without proper supervision.

Since our children, their children and their children's children represent the future and whatever hope there is for mankind, what can we do to alter the situation and bring about change. Do we stand on the sidelines and say "Its in God's hands. I have faith. The Lord will provide".

There is another saying; "The Lord helps those who help themselves".

The picture is not entirely bleak. There are many wholesome, loving and caring families who maintain stable home environments and actively participate in their offspring's development. Unfortunately, these do not make the headlines. For those others who make the evening news in a negative fashion, there is much that we can do.

Whatever your political persuasion, put pressure on members of state and national government bodies to enact beneficial legislation.

The crime bill recently passed calls for the death penalty for 60 federal crimes, for more jails and policemen, for three strikes and you are out;. (Life imprisonment for the third felony conviction). As originally proposed, it had provisions for crime prevention, job training programs, drug education and treatment and recreational activities. The money for these programs was drastically reduced by filibustering conservatives who mouthed the old slogans about socialism, pork barrels and tax and spend liberals while continuously endorsing excessive star wars defense spending by the pentagon and vigorously supporting the National Rifle Association in its efforts to prevent any form of gun control. Health care reform is in limbo and may possibly be watered down to meaningless change because the AMA, pharmaceutical companies, HMO;s and Insurance companies are spending millions of dollars in ads filled with false and misleading information and making lobbying contributions to congressmen who support their propaganda.

So get involved in elections to help insure victory for those candidates who support positive programs. Let your views be known to those already in office. Help set up day care centers and supervised play areas for children of working parents, Visit schools and discuss your child's education progress with teachers and administrators. Set up neighborhood crime watches and help protect each others property. Promptly report any suspicious characters in the area or residences where unusual activity such as drug dealing may transpire. Be willing to serve on boards and committees in your communities and churches. Become a big Brother or Sister to kids in need of positive role models.

Obviously these suggestions will not be a cure all for the ills of society, nor will they guarantee that the future will be safer and brighter, but they will be a small step in the right direction.

Above all, as you work diligently for positive change, keep the faith.

Thank you.

Family History July 3, 1996

In early June when I sent out the newsletter to family members, I included a letter in the one to Daisy Westry, Uncle Joe's daughter in San Francisco.

I reviewed some of the comments Uncle Joe had made about the family during an afternoon visit we made in February, and requested that she try to stimulate his memory for further details and some additional questions that had come to mind.

The Church of the Latter Day Saints (Morman) in Loudenville, New York, about 4 miles North of Albany, has a family history center and can order microfilms from the major church in Salt Lake City, Utah, which has a vast file of families from all around the world. About 3 weeks ago I visited the facility in New York state and spent several hours discussing family data with one of the research assistants. I explained my inability to locate any data on my great grandmother, Caroline Crawford and 6 of her 7 children except for the 1870 census, Peter, our grandfather, was listed in most subsequent documents, He suggested that `I order the microfiln of marriage records for Estill County Kentucky from the mid 1800's to 1900. He also had some suggestions for things to look up at the Silvio Conte National Archives.

Microfilm rental plus postage is paid in advance and takes about 3 weeks for delivery to the local church. I received a postcard on Monday, July 1 informing me that the film was in and would be held up to 3 weeks before being returned. So Tuesday I drove over and in about 10 minutes discovered that there was no useful information on it. There were only 4 Crawfords and 2 Stagners listed, none of whom had familiar family names. I did spend a couple of hours looking at other data about blacks and reading several articles.

Returning to the Silvio Conte Archives in Pittsfield, I followed one suggestion of the assistant; that I look up Emma Duncan in the Soundex for the 1980 census. The records for that year only list households with children under 10 years of age. And Emma, born in December, 1877 would have been 2 in the Spring of 1880. In rolling through all of the Duncans in Mobile County, I came across a Thomas Dunkan. (Inconsistent spelling of names was a common occurence as many blacks recently released from slavery could neither read nor write, and many immigrants could not speak English, so the census taker wrote down whatever the name sounded like phonetically.)

Thomas was 60 years old and his wife Sarah, was 26, Obviously she wasn't the mother of all the children as the oldest, Thomas, the only son, was 15. Four daughters were listed: Eldelias 11, Irine 8, Roxyanna 5, and Emma 2. checking with Ruth in the family Bible revealed that all the names were present except Eldelias and that the father was listed as Samuel, not Thomas. Hopefully, back up documentation for this and several other questions can be answered when I go to Mobile on August 4th for 3 days.

I will be a delegate from the Greater Boston Tuskegee Club at the Alumni Conference August 7-11, and plan to fly in and out of Mobile. I will rent a car for the trip to and from Tuskegee University.

I have had several correspondences and faxes with the Probate court in Mobile and have received the marriage license of Frank Wright and Emma Duncan, and a listing of deed records for the Wrights and Martha Crawford. These and other vital statistics will be pursued during my 3 day sojourn. I also hope to locate some of the family sites and photograph the changes that have taken place.

Some of you are wondering, "Why go to all this trouble and expenditure of time and money?" I can only say that after 2 years of research as a volunteer and Friend of the Archives and Publicity Chairman on the board, the bug bites you. The more you learn, the more questions arise and the more you want to know. There are hundreds of people who put in far more hours than I do at the research center and they all express similar sentiments.

It is a fascinating challenge and a never ending quest.

Mobile and Tuskegee Revisited

On August 14, 1994, after spending four days in Orlando with my wife Rosemary, daughter, Rosemary Smith and her two children, Richard and Vanessa, I headed for Alabama in my Plymouth Voyager to show them the area in which the family had spent some of our early years. My wife and I had returned over the same route in 1974 following a Chrie Conference in Miami. Completing the 500 mile drive by early evening, I stopped at a phone booth to look up the number and address of Barbara Wright, the widow of Uncle Ed. She was delighted following identification, to know that "Junior" was in town and gave instructions for reaching her new abode Unfortunately, my description of the location was incorrect and we had to stop at a store and get the proper heading.

Barbara was waiting outside by the street when we arrived and happy to meet my family. Going inside we chatted about the old days on the farm and the ordeal surrounding the birth of her first born son, Edward, Jr. (As mentioned in the family history, he suffered irreversible brain damage when she was in labor for many hours before being taken to a hospital for a cesarean section delivery) Barbara was always a short very tiny woman and now at 79 years of age, looked even more petite. She was 19 when they got married. Although in his 50's, Edward still goes regularly to a rehab center. A big gentle fellow, he bears a strong resemblance to his father who died July 3, 1968 at the age of 78.

Her former residence on McRae Ave. had been ruined in a flood following heavy rains the year before. Hence, her new location.

I got out my video camera and took a picture of Barbara and Ed Jr. before departing. She gave instructions for the route to take to Pritchard and Whistler but after about half an hour of driving up and down the road looking for familiar streets, our exhausted family decided to return to Mobile and find a motel for the night. Accomodations were made at the Red Roof Inn on I-65 which leads from Mobile to Montgomery.

Monday morning, as an early riser, I left while they were still sleeping to look for familiar landmarks. I found the New Light and Mount Sinai Baptist Churches and Boaz Avenue and Bearfork Road. Returning to the Red Roof, the car was loaded and we went back to Whistler. The first stop was 720 Boaz Ave. where Irma and her son, Henry lived. Irma was still in Harrisburg, PA with her daughter, Delores, but Henry was spotted mowing the lawn. He was introduced to the family and after a brief conversation, agreed to having his picture taken. He was in work clothes and sweaty. I also took pictures of the exterior of the house and discussed the visit in 1974 when my wife and I stayed for a few days with Irma and her husband, Louis Caleb, and Louis had showed his maniken demonstration of the crucifixion. Henry told us the approximate location of the former family farm but did not offer to lead the way. Driving out Bear Fork Road, now paved and lined with residences and about a dozen churches, I discussed the area of the 1930s and the 3 mile walk into town.

I drove down several offshooting roads but was unable to locate the trail through the woods mentioned by Henry. So returning to I-65 North, we headed for Montgomery and picked up I-85 for Tuskegee.

The road to the campus passed Moton Field and I pointed out where I had taken flight training during my Senior year in 1948.

The new multimillion dollar Kellogg Conference Center which was under construction last year during my 45th reunion had been completed and reservations were made to spend the night there. Ten of these conference centers are located in the United States, but this is the only one located on a black college campus. It contains a fitness center, a swimming pool and a restaurant, several floors of rooms, an auditorium and a parking garage.

After checking in and getting settled, the family set out on a walking tour of a portion of the hugh campus to be followed by a driving tour and a visit to the off campus community. The first stop was the George Washington Carver Museum adjacent to the conference center. In the years that I had spent at Tuskegee, I had never visited the museum before.

Many of the pictures and artifacts were captured on videotape. I showed them where my training in the culinary field had taken place and the site where Pearl and I had attended our last year of high school. The building had burned down a few years ago and a new high school had been constructed off campus. Next, we saw the administration building, library, science building, gymnasium, stadium, alumni house, Booker T. Washington's residence, dormitories and chapel. A drive around the campus showed the Vetinary Medical Center, School of Engineering, School of Agriculture and the former Lewis Adams Elementary School where Ruth, Jerry and Marie had been students for two years.

Leaving the campus for Greenwood, they were shown the Greenwood Baptist Church, a new brick building across the street from the location when the family attended, the two houses in which the Crawfords had resided, and the house in which Rosemary and I had resided in 1947 before I got an apartment in the married veterans housing complex. We also drove out to the Veterans Hospital where Isaac, Sr. had spent about a month in 1939, and I told them something of the history of this formerly all black hospital (staff and patients).

Returning to Kellogs, Richard, Vanessa and I worked out in the fitness center and then they and their mother took a swim in the pool. The dining room was checked out as a possible dinner site but I couldn't see spending that kind of money, especially with two kids who preferred hamburgers.

So we headed for downtown Tuskegee and discovered that the only eating establishments were of the fast food variety. We settled for Kentucky Fried Chicken. The next morning, August 16th, we had the buffet breakfast at the center, checked out and began the long trek home.

It had rained off and on during the four days spent in Florida. A tropical storm was moving up from the Gulf and heavy rain was forecast along with the possibility of tornados, Luckily, despite the heavy and persistent rain, the tornados did not catch up. They struck South Carolina about an hour after we had passed through and warnings were issued for North Carolina. That night was spent in Chester, VA at the Days Inn. The room rate included a buffer breakfast.

On the 17th, following a drive into Washington, D C, the kids were shown the historical sites: Jefferson Memorial, Washington Monument, The Mall, White House and Capital building.

A call was placed to the residence of Juletta and Charles Smith in Silver Springs, Maryland to ascertain directions and several hours were spent visiting with them. Charles was at work but came home after a call from Juletta. She was quite sore having been recently involved in an automobile accident. Chris, their youngest son, had just returned from the Woodstock concerts in upstate New York. The Smiths lived in Pittsfield in the late sixties and early seventies when Charles, a retired Army Colonel, was employed at General Electric. I invited them to a dinner at First Baptist Church and they subsequently became members, joined the choir and became very active in church and community affairs. Juletta taught art in the Pittsfield school system and continued in the Washington area when they moved.

A neighbor of theirs in Silver Springs had been an instructor in the ROTC program in the 1950's. He was invited over to meet the Crawfords and it was discovered that he and I had both served in the Navy in the South Pacific during World War 11.

Juletta suggested staying for dinner and overnight, but feeling that 3 adults and 2 children would be quite an imposition, I declined and we left for home around 4 p m, stopping for dinner along the way and arriving home at 1 A M. after driving through torrential downpours.

Total mileage, 3,402.8

The Rest of The Story

I had applied for entrance into the training program for Master Gardeners when I retired in 1989, but was informed that funding for the program had been dropped by the state. In 1995 formerly trained gardeners decided to reactivate the program by having applicants pay a fee to cover costs of hiring instructors from the Conservation district and University of MA in Amherst. I was accepted and completed the 12 weeks of classes plus 60 hours of volunteering by doing soil tests,manning the hot line for gardening questions at Smith College and Berkshire Botannical Gardens to answer questions from homeowners. Having spent much of my childhood on the farm and gardened for much of my adult life, I realized how wasteful and time consuming trial and error methods were, and wanted the knowledge and skill to make the right decisions and use the proper techniques. I created a 12 bed raised vegetable garden, several perennial and annual flower plots, and bulb beds, blusberry and raspberry bushes, 2 pear trees, 4 apple trees and dozens of shrubs and bushes and evergreens.

Over the years constant changes have been made to the house and landscape. The pond was started years ago by digging a straight bipass for the brook and bulldozing out the old zigzag brook bed. Two dozen large pine trees on the south side of the house were removed in 1980 to allow sunlight for gardening and flowers. I added a passive solar room and use it to start plants from seed for the vegetables and flower beds. I also raise tropical plants such as pineapple, poinsettias, coleus, impatience,

Begonias,etc., which are potted and placed outside for the Summer. Rosemary has dozens of indoor plants which she propogates.

Also, in 1990, I replaced the roof over the house. Although I did all of the lining up and nailing of the slates, My Grandson, Eric, frequently came out to bring up the ladder some of the 90 + packages of roofing.

Rosemary has quit working in surgery. Relegated to part time and being on call meant she had to remain in the area in case she was buzzed for an emergency. She became active in a number of community and church organizations. She became director of volunteers for the auxillary at Hillcrest Hospital and served a term on the Board of Directors. At Church she was president of the Women's League for many years and a member of the Memorial-Historical Committee. She is currently chair of that committee and the church clerk; and is a member of the Pittsfield Area Council of Churches and Church Women United. She also bowls in the Senior League for retirees. She has served as camera operator on some of my shows and on the TV committee at church where our worship services are broadcast live each Sunday.

We were on a two week vacation in February of 1996 to visit Isaac Allen and his family in San Jose California when an unexpected emergency occured. Rosemary woke up one morning with pain in her arm and attributed it to the fact that she may have slept on it during the night. This was the day before we were scheduled to return home, so, since she seemed all right, I left for a final round of golf before going back to the Berkshire winter weather with its unusually heavy snowfall. Luckily, our son had not yet departed for work. The pain increased in intensity, and began to move up her arm. She also began to feel hot and sweaty. Having worked in surgery and seen some of the emergencies, plus having recently attended a program in which a cardiac nurse with lecture and slides presented a graphic picture of the symptoms preceding cardiac arrest, responded to Isaac's query "Are you alright?", with, "I think you had better take me to the hospital". They hastily made the 10 mile trip to Good Samaritan Hospital where she was treated in the emergency room with nitro and other appropiate drugs and a series of tests set up. While she had not gone into cardiac arrest, the dye test found three blocked arteries. They were deemed too severly constricted to respond to angioplasty so bypass surgery was scheduled for two days hence. If she was going to have heart surgery, this was the ideal time and place as compared to back home where one had to go to Albany, Worcester or Boston, and sometimes wait weeks to schedule an operation. An entire wing of the enormous structure was devoted to cardiac care; from emergency entrance, pre-operative, surgical and intensive care, to post operative recuperation on an upper floor with rooftop flower gardens outside the windows. Also, some of the best cardiologists and surgeons had offices along the street adjacent to the hospital. Her surgeon had two full time cardiac nurses who met with patients and their family members to offer reassurance, explain each step of the procedure and answer any questions. They also would come to the waiting room to give a status report to anxious family members during the lengthy four hour operation. Rosemary ended up with a quadruple bypass. They found a fourth blocked aterey. Replacement vessels were taken from breast and down the thigh. Isaac Allen and I were allowed to see her in intensive care about an hour after surgery. We were shocked at all the tubes and clamps, and had to hold her arms to prevent her from yanking out the tube down her throat while the nurse got restraints and tied her arms down. She explained that it would be much worse to reinsert the tube. After a night in ICU, Rosemary was moved upstairs for four days before being released. Metal pins had been inserted in her sternum to hold the bones in place and would remain there permanently. To help ease the pain caused by coughing, she was given a small pillow to hug tightly to her chest.

Following such a drastic invasion and shock to the body, she was too weak to bathe or dress for several more days and took several months to feel like her old self again. We came home two weeks later and about six weeks later she began a rehab program at BMC. Doctors and nurses here marveled at the size of her scar which was only about one third that of patients who go to hospitals in the area. She had smoked for most of her life and enjoyed a high fat diet and lots of salt. The cardiologist in California said the blockage had been taken care of and would be effective for a number of years; but the length really depended on her. She immediately threw her cigarettes away. and quit smoking. Some changes were made in her diet, but she lacks the will power to give up luncheon meats, cheeses, and butter spread on bread, vegetables and starches. and ice cream and cookies.

I had been named vice moderator of First Baptist Church and shortly after we returned from California, the moderator suffered a slight heart attack while vacationing in New Hampshire. I was asked to accept the position until the next election and have been chairing meetings of the executive council, the church council, and the annual all church meeting. Our minister, Dr. David Johnson Rowe, replaced Dale Lock, who served for 25 years and died of Prostate Cancer in 1992, Rev. Rowe and his wife, Bonnie, have both worked diligently to move the church forward with increased membership, greater youth involvement, dynamic preaching, summer programs, Bible studies, etc.; but in the process have alienated the affections of some disgruntled members who have resigned from the church. Others have remained but have often been blatant and abusive in criticism, often over trivia. So after three years, he has tendered his resignation, effective May 31, 1997. That is two weeks after we celebrate the 225th annniversary of the founding of the church. One wonders sometimes how we can call ourselves "Christians".

It should be said however, that David's primary objective, in spite of all the good ideas and programs was in building a resume that would look good to prospective jobs in other churches. He accepted a position as Senior Pastor at a church in Fairfield, CT with a larger and wealthier congregation.

The floor project was finally started in July and finished in September. Originally, Rosemary had planned to go visit Isaac in California and it was my intention to work on the floor while she was gone. The trip was cancelled when it was discovered that Gwen's relatives would be there at that time. This was an advantage, because her assistance was invaluable in moving and storing all of the furniture, appliances and knick knacks from the living and dining rooms. My first plan was to just do the living room and hallways since we had replaced the dining room carpet a few years ago. But it didn't make much sense to have the flooring end in a straight line at the wide archway to the dining room and then, a few years later, do that room. So all of the carpeting and underlay were removed along with the nails and staples. Loose and uneven areas of the subfloor were repaired and an underlay of resin paper put down. 28 boxes of 20 square feet each of Bruce prefinished oak flooring was ordered and delivered from Home Depot in West Springfield. A manually operated Porter nailer and hammer were rented from Carr Hardware and three boxes of special nails were purchased. My golfing buddy, Richard Halvorsen, came by to help me lay a plumb line and start the first two rows of flooring.

Like many of the home and grounds projects that I have undertaken for the first time, there was a misconception concerning the amount of time and effort required and the problems and difficulties to be encountered. Although the boards were of varying lengths, it was not always possible to lay out a combination that would reach from end to end without cutting and sometimes chiseling and/or sanding to fit around projections of wall ends. Also a space of about 1/2 inch was recommended at each wall to allow for expansion and contraction caused by temperature and humidity variations. I worked about 10 hours each day that first Friday, Saturday and Sunday, and then had to take a week off to allow my legs and back to get back in shape. After that, a more sensible schedule was followed. Work a few hours, do other projects for a while, and then work a few more hours.

Upon completion of the two rooms, the floor was cleaned and the furniture put back. A colorful carpet was purchased for the dining room but it proved to be too small to allow for moving chairs to and from the table without coming in contact with the wood flooring. So I cut the former carpeting to a size that was satisfactory and allowed the wood flooring to be visible all around it. The unused rug was added to the other area rug in the living room.

It was necessary to buy three more boxes of flooring plus long runners for the hallways. The folding doors on the hall closet were replaced with sliding ones. A wrought iron fence along the cellar stairwell was replaced by an oaken one. With her precision routing equipment, Eleanor drilled the holes, and I glued and screwed the railing and poles together and stained and varnished them.

We still have to tackle the cellar. It is such a waste of space to have the entire area filled with things we no longer use or want. Unfortunately, with the new disposal system in effect in Dalton, it will cost a small fortune to pay for the loads of items not capable of being recycled. Under the old landfill system of a few years ago, this could have been done easily and cheaply. So much for procrastination. And even the things we value will probably be added to the "get rid of" list by our heirs upon our inevitable termination.

My next major project was the driveway, which was a mixture of gravel and soil and full of weeds, which required several applications of roundup per season. I used a prong rake to loosen the weeds and gravel; picked out as many weeds as possible, then sifted the gravel to capture the soil for filling in areas of the front yard that were low, or had tree roots that were above ground and got hit by the mower. I widened the two car entrance in front of the garage and the semi-circular driveway with two exits or entrances. The gravel was leveled in place and topped with 22 tons of Airport mix, a blue stone mix that compacted when leveled, wet down and pressed. also a walkway was made through the gravel to the back door. For the first year, everything was great. But this year a few weeds have sprouted. Probably the heavy record setting rain we have experienced this summer of 2,000 washed out the acidity of the mixture and allowed weed seeds to germinate. There are a few spots that gather water and some scanty fill near the roadway. So I will probably buy another ton or two and redo these areas plus the walkway to the back door.

During the Fall of 99, I got my usual flu shot from the visiting Nurses Association which provides the free shots for the elderly at the Community Center in Dalton. Unfortunately, a different strain hit the area and many people came down with a serious illiness that lasted about ten days and several died of complications and pneumonia. On Christmas Eve morning, I walked out to get the paper after suffering chills and fever during the night. Returning, I went to the bathroom and feeling weird, sat down on the toilet seat. The next thing I heard was several people calling my name and pulling me to my feet. Rosemary had called 911 after she heard me fall and was unable to lift me. Our neighbor across the street, Smith, who is an auxillary policeman, had heard the call on his scanner and was the first to arrive. Two ambulances responded because they thought I had had a heart attack and Dalton did not have all of the technical equipment. They had me out in the cold on the porch while they checked all my vital signs before placing me in the ambulance and driving to the hospital. there they did an EKG, blood tests and X-rays while I explained to them that I had the flu. finally I warmed up sufficiently for my temperature to rise to about 100 F. (My normal is about 97.8) They suggested that I stay in the hospital, which I rejected. So they gave me a prescription to have filled when Rosemary drove me home. I was very weak for 5 or 6 days and it took a few more days to get up to full strength. But I knew that I didn't wish to remain in bed and develop pneumonia. One of my golfing buddies died that same week at the hospital. He had been a great tennis player and bowler, and still walked the golf course in his eighties; but pneumonia did him in.

Eric Wilder's father, Rosemary's first husband, Charles Wider, was killed in an automobile accident over the Christmas holidays enroute from Connecticut to the Berkshires. He was 52.

Our nephew and Godson, Eric Crawford, adopted son of Jerry and his first wife, Gladys Lewis, came by Saturday night, January 13, 2001, with his current significant other. It was the night of his 40th bithday and they had been visiting in Pittsfield and gone to dinner at the Country Buffet. Eric has been virtually disowned by his father because of numerous misdeeds in his youth. Although he claims to have altered his habits and lifestyle, we take whatever he says with a grain of salt. We have pemitted him to stay in our house a few days over the years, but are wary of leaving him alone in the house. So when he asked if he could stay a few days this week, and stated that he would provide a food allowance, since he was a big eater during previous visits, I truthfully told him that we both had committments in various groups and organizations and would frequently be away from home: Church, bowling, Studio, Archives, meetings, etc., and it wasn't a good idea. He agreed and they departed around 10:30 p.m.

We have had the coldest November and December on record. For 20 days in December the temperature never rose above freezing. This would mean a small fortune in fuel oil costs if that was my only source of heat. Luckily, three dying maples along the street in front of the house were approved for removal by the tree warden, and I had the opportunity to cut, split, stack and haul. Our neighbor, Vinnie Donovan, a fellow golfer and bowler, loaned me his log splitter and that was used for most of the larger trunk sections. I stacked the wood over in the Northeast section of the front yard along the property line under the pines, and brought it in as necessary when my supply dwindled. With the extremly cold weather, I would be be about out by now except for a Christmas present from Rosemary and Isaac of a cord of wood. That should take me well into February. The wood boiler is set up to be the current supplier of heat and hot water, with the furnace only coming on when the water temperature drops below a certain level, as when the fire is dying or out. An additional benefit of the wood burning is the amount of physical exercise (labor) required. With a heavy layer of snow on the ground I have had to shovel and pack a path to the back door, and use the wheelbarrow instead of the tractor and trailer to haul wood. I have tried to keep the south wall under the solar room stacked to the ceiling with wood just in case weather conditions prohibit those trips. Then its several wheel barrows full into the playroom where the stove is located and stacking that rack for a two day supply. About a dozen times a day it is necessary to go up and down the stairs to refuel the fire, and once a day remove the ashes and take them outside to cool down before disposal. So far this Winter, I have gained only 5 pounds instead of my usual 15. With Walking 3 mornings per week at the mall and bowling 3 afternoons, this is probably the best shape for the winter in a long time.

I will miss about 6 days of bowling because I agreed to videotape the Master Gardener classes on 6 Thursdays. The entire schedule was recorded for the 1997 class, but these tapes are of the classes with different material or new instructors. Thursday, Jan.19th was my first one. Four of us from the Berkshires carpooled from Coltsville behind the Pizza Hut at 7:a.m. and returned at 4:30 p.m., which makes for a long day. It takes 3 tapes to record the 2 classes of 2-1/2 hours each, plus more to do the editing and make copies for the Gardener's Library. These tapes plus the old ones are available to any of the fifty students who mght have to miss a class. Two misses is all that is allowed. In addition to refreshing my memory and increasing my knowledge of various sciences, I get material for Ike's Forum on Dalton Community TV. It also increases my volunteer hours for RSVP, (9 hours yesterday and 3 today).

My Physical activity came to a temporary conclusion Sunday night, January 28, 2001. I had been feeling some pain and soreness in the groin and upper thigh area since hauling all that wood in the wheelbarrow a couple of weeks ago. And Friday morning when I did my usual 30 minute brisk walk at the mall, It became more painful to put all my weight on the left leg. By Sunday, I was limping as I tried to walk naturally. At the Annual meeting when I had to rise about a dozen times and go to the mike, It became more painful. For the rest of the day and early evening, the pain was constant whether standing, sitting, or lying down. I got my crutches out and tried hobbling down the hallway. Shortly after going to bed a little after 11p.m., and lying there in agony, I decided to go to the Emergency Room for diagnosis and treatment. Rosemary had been sleeping through all of this, and I decided not to wake her, but to leave a note in case she woke up before I returned. After leg manipulation, x-rays and poking here and there it was decided that I had a torn muscle and that the abnormal moving and walking had caused the Sciatic Nerve to react with pain running down the leg. I was asked to rate the pain on a scale from 1 to 1O. I gave it an 8. It was suggested that I refrain from any strenuous activity for a week and continue to use the crutches. Three types of pills were prescribed: one for pain, one to reduce swellng and one to help me sleep. Two days later, there seems to be some improvement though getting comfortable in bed is virtually impossible. I did go downstairs to shut down the wood boiler and to adjust the temperature controls on the furnace so that it would supply more heat and hot water. The last delivery of oil required only 29 gallons, so the wood burning was a tremendous saving.

By Thursday afternoon the pain had dissipated and I could put my weight on the leg and walk normally. I thought everything was fine, but about mid morning Friday, I began to develop a severe headache and feel a little groggy. Checking my blood pressure, it was 174/106. Believing that my checker was not working properly, I asked Rosemary to check with hers, and the reading was slightly higher. Fearing the consequences of a possible stroke, I called my primary care Physician's office and was informed that they were swamped and an appointment would not be available until Monday, even after I explained the seriousness of the situation. (Dr. Taylor wil no longer be my Doctor.) The decision was then made to go to the

Emergency Room, but Rosemary suggested that we try her Cardiac Care Physician, Dr. McNulty. So we went there first and were told he would see me but we would have to wait a while. After about an hour I received his attention. My pressure was now 196/ 110 and he said there was some edema in my legs. (That could have been because he was feelng the thick winter socks I was wearing.) An EKG revealed no problems with the heart and the lungs were fine. He gave me a 28 day supply of blood pressure reducing pills (lrbesartan-hYdrochlorathiazide) brand name, Avalide, and scheduled an appointment on Feb. 12th to check the Carotid Arteries. A nurse drew four vials of blood for checking Cholesterol, Glucose level, PSA for Prostate, etc. and I had to leave a sample of Urine. After taking a pill a day for two days the pressure dropped to the 170's and low 90's. I will continue to monitor it daily and when it reaches acceptable levels, the drugs will be discontinued. Like all medications the possible side effects can be scary. I will try bowling tomorrow and, if that works out okay, will resume more of my activities. Surely, one of the saddest things in life is the job that old age begins to do to your body no matter how careful you are about diet and exercise and physical fitness.

To add to my misfortunes, I was bringing in a few loads of wood from the remaining pile by the garage late Friday afternoon and decided to get the mail before my last load. I decided to put the mail in the solar room because there was too much to fit in my jacket pocket. I had to walk around the wheelbarrow and down the slope beside the garage door. As I put my right foot on the slope it suddenly slid forward on the ice under the snow and I felt myself falling backward. My head grazed the corner of the garage and I landed on my back. Slowly rising to my feet, I discovered that my left arm could not be extended horizontally or vertically without considerable pain. After a couple of days of pain and restless nights I decided to call the Doctor who had been conducting my bienniel physical exams for flying. It was President's Day and I only got a message from his answering service. The next day his office scheduled an appointment at the hospital for X-rays which revealed no broken bones. He gave me some sample pain medication (Tramadol HCL tablets) and suggested that I make an appointment with my Orthopaedic surgeon to review the situation. My appointment is for March 13th. The Tramadol was supposed to be taken about an hour before retiring for the night. My first pill caused severe side effects: naseau, disorientation, weakness, tingling skin, etc. So that was the only pill I took. The pain has persisted in my shoulder and arm. I have been spending only about five hours in bed per night for the past few years because of my inability to sleep on my back because of the post nasal drip which leads to choking and gagging. Now with one bad shoulder, I can only sleep on my right side.

Thus I drowse in a chair in my office as I read, watch TV or do crossword puzzles until about midnight.

I have been able to resume bowling and my game is getting back to normal as I can partially help support the ball at a low angle with my left hand. Yesterday, I had my best series of the year with 228, 183, 203 for a 614 total. I have also resumed walking at the Mall between 5 and 6 a.m. several days per week. The pain can be felt in the shoulder if I move that arm too much, but one gets used to discomfort after a few weeks, and hopefully, some healing begins to occur.

Continuing the saga of possible physical infirmities, yesterday, March 7th, I had an appointment with Dr. Noyes, a Uroligist who joined the firm of Mamonas and Kavorkis, before their retirement. Surprisingly, I spent more time trying to find a parking space in the parking garage adjacent to the hospital and medical center than I did waiting for the Doctor. This was quite a departure from the usual hour or more wait and I mentioned it to the Nurse who said they try to be different. This visit was as a result of my elevated PSA blood test regarding the prostate gland. During the question and answer period regarding symptoms and previous history, I mentioned the T.U.R. (Transurethal resection) perfomed by Dr. Mamonas in 1980. Dr. Noyes said that surgery was probably one of the last performed by Mamonas as he retired that year and moved to Florida. He is still alive and in his 90's. I also had a rectal ultrasound check of the prostate by Dr. Vasakas about 6 years ago before his retirement.

Dr. Noyes did a cursory exam of my genitals and lower abdomen and then a finger probe of the Prostate through the rectum. His probe was so searching that it felt like he was poking a hole through the intestinal wall. He then said to get cleaned up and dressed and he would be back to talk in a few minutes. He said the prostate was still small and Dr. Mamonas had done a good job. But the rectal exam could only probe the top surface of the prostate, which he found to be quite hard. He would schedule an ultrasound to more closely examine the area and reveal any abnormalities, and remove tissue for a biopsy. My next appointment is March 27th at 10 a.m. The aide who scheduled it gave me a brown bag of medication and instructions to prepare for that moment. Take a Levaquin 500 mg tablet the night before. Take one Fleet enema 2 hours before the exam. Eat a light breakfast or lunch before the exam, then limit intake to clear liquids. Drink 2 glasses of water one hour before the appointment, and do not urinate after drinking the water. A partially full bladder will allow the doctor to see the prostate more clearly. (This is easier said than done. When I have to go, which is frequently, there is no holding back.) Plan to spend 30 minutes to 1 hour in the Ultrasound Department.

After spending three hours snowblowing on Tuesday morning to get a pathway through the 16-18 inches of snow and be able to use the driveway, my shoulder is feeling the twinges. I had thought of canceling my appointment with the orthopaedist for next Wednesday after having to wait almost three weeks to have it checked out. But, for the sake of finding out the true extent of injury and damage to the joint and surrounding tissue, I guess I will keep the appointment.

The Noreaster did not turn out to be one of the greatest of the past century as predicted, but it did cause considerable problems and cancellations, many of them premature. All schools were canceled Sunday night in anticipation of the storm starting after midnight. Also many businesses and government offices were closed. In reality, despite the dire weather predictions on every TV and radio channel, only a light coating of sleet and snow fell until late Monday afternoon when the real snowfall started and lasted until about 7 a.m. Tuesday. By the time several trips had been made by the town snow plow, there was a 3 foot high wall of snow at the end of the driveway. I put on my knee high boots when I went out to get the paper and found that they weren't high enough as snow went over the top and down inside as I struggled with each step in the 16 inches of soft snow. By the time I got back inside the workout was about the same as walking a couple of miles at the Mall. I had to change clothes as the pajama pant legs, and the bottom of my robe and coat were all coated and soaked with snow. Some video shots of the snow scenes were taken as proof of the depth. On Friday we got another foot of snow. This is getting ridiculous. This three foot build up serves to enhance the probability of severe flooding as the warm weather and rain approach.

My March 13th appointment with Dr. Cohen took place yesterday. He had all my files from previous contact with the firm starting with the Carpal Tunnel Syndrome surgery by Dr. Slowick and included his own sutures on my left arm at the emergency room at BMC. He had just joined Orthopaedic Associates and happened to be at the hospital when I came in with a gash created by tapping the arm with a chain saw while removing limbs from a fallen tree. X-rays revealed no bone damage to my shoulder, but by manipulating the arm in several directions and causing increased pain, he said it might be a torn rotator cuff. An MRI would be necessary to verify or rule out that possibility. Also it would be necessary to have continued exercise of the shoulder, or it would freeze up and be permanently disabled. He scheduled the MRI for next Wednesday night, March 21st and arranged for a therapist to call me and set up an appointment for manipulation. Dr Cohen said if the Rotator cuff is torn and requires surgery, it would take about a year to heal completely. Let's hope he is wrong. I have already sent in my dues for Wahconah this year. I did not tell him that the arm stays in use: bowling, driving, shoveling and blowing snow, using a roof rake to remove some of the snow from the lower edge of the roof, walking at the mall and swinging the arm a litle more each time. the pain is greatest when the arm is turned as in putting on, or removing a shirt or jacket, and in laying in bed. Dr. Cohen said he couldn't believe that I was almost 77 years old. I told him that was one of my problems when I visited my family physician. He would marvel at my muscular structure and talk about great genes instead of doing a complete physical.

Today, March 31, 2001, Dr. Noyes gave me the news re my biopsy on the 27th. There are cancer cells in my prostate. Because the PSA blood test was only 5.5, he doesn't believe the cancer has metastasized (spread), but he will schedule a bone scan to determine the facts. A hormone will be given to reduce the testosterone level and the size of the prostate, making a more favorable target for the radiation treatment which he recommends. He said the two choices are surgical removal or radiation. For younger men, surgery is recommended since they have a longer life expectancy. For those over 75 with a ten to twelve year expectancy, radiation is the preferred treatment. Well at least it was benign when I had the TUR 21 years ago, so I guess I should be thankful for those 21 years of good health.

The bone scan from head to toe was negative. The cancer cells had not spread. Dr. Noyes gave me the hormone injection and explained that it would perform a chemical castration as opposed to the old method of removal of the testicles. (I seem to recall my father had his removed, but I don't know the details.) In about 3 weeks I would begin to experience hot flashes: the male menopause. An appointment was set up with the Radiation Oncologist for April 20th.

I spent about two hours at the hospital this morning. the female assistant to the Oncologist came out to the waiting area and took me in for an interview and some discussion of lifestyle. She had me undress and put on the traditional gown for an exam by the doctor. We discussed bowling friends of mine, 3 Dillie Boys, who have successfully had the treatment in recent years and she gave me a pamphlet of the Prostate Support Group of the Berkshires who meet monthly to share experiences and have a guest speaker. Dr. Sheridan checked heart, lungs, lymph nodes and abdomen, and then did a rectal probe of the prostate. He said the hormone was probably working because the tissue was soft. I got dressed and went into his office for a long discussion of the scale of my cancer and the optimum treatment. On a rating of 1 to 10, on the Gleason Scale, mine was about a 2. Six to nine is more serious. He used the word cure instead of remission, and said that the modern use of the catscan and computer can pinpoint the exact location of the cancer cells and block out the site for radiation; and treatment 5 days per week for about 6-1/2 weeks should complete the cure. He scheduled the catscan and imaging for May 29th saying he wanted to wait about two months for the hormone to do its work before starting radiation. I then had to go to the lab for a blood test. Somewhat perplexed, I was a little upset regarding the 2 month delay before starting treatment There is a tendency to want matters taken care of immediately when a potentially serious medical problem is discovered. But one has to rely on the "expertise" of the specialist regarding treatment.

In reviewing the above text it was discovered that I hadn't mentioned another mishap which caused considerable discomfort and financial loss. A couple of months ago Rosemary bought a hide-a-bed at a church tag sale for the other bedroom. This is a folding single bed that opens up into a double. I removed the two rear seats from the van and went to First Baptist to pick it up. In order to hold the bed down in place, the two fellows who helped me, put masking tape on each end. Eric came out to help me bring it into the house and set it up. We stood the bed on its side and started to remove the tape. Suddenly it sprang out and whacked me in the jaw, breaking two teeth: a top incisor and a lower premolar. Half of the incisor was snapped off and the molar was cracked and lost its filling. The Dentist, Glen Burgner, had to do a root canal job on the incisor, insert a steel pin and put on a temporary cap. There wasn't enough tooth left to support a cap for biting. He had to cut away the gum line around the molar to reveal the extent of the damage, and allow several weeks for healing before installing a temporary cap. I am scheduled to go back on May 3rd for the next step. The total cost will probably run about $2,000 over the dental insurance limit. All for an $85 bed.

It is June 2, 2001. I went to BMC on Tuesday, the 29th of May for a cat scan to pinpoint the exact location of the cancer cells for external beam radiation. The technician molded a cast for my legs and had me lie on my stomach with my face down in a plastic hole in a "pillow". He then proceded to tattoo the exact spots where the beam would enter on my hips and buttocks and drew circles and a line. One has to be perfectly still as this imaging takes place. Any necessary movement is done by him as he tugs the mat on which the patient lies, he said the treatment would start in a couple of days. They would call me. I asked for the earliest time possible, which is 7:30 a.m. opening, since I am involved in golf and other activities and appointments during the day. When they hadn't called by Friday, I called them in the afternoon and the receptionist in the Oncology Department said I could start Monday at 7:30. Then she called back later and said they were switching to a different machine and all the morning slots were filled. So I will be going at 2:30. A regular schedule for the six weeks will be worked out later.

No wonder medical costs are skyrocketing and HMO's are leaving the Berkshires. Yesterday's mail brought two invoices from Blue Cross-Blue Shield. One from Berkshire Urological Associates, Dr. Noyes, was $133 for the office visit and $2,343 for the hormone shot, labeled chemotherapy. Medicare paid $82.75 and $1,339.47 respectively; and Blue Cross-Blue Shield said the usual response, "We cannot pay this claim because this particular service is not covered under your contract". This probably accounts for why the school district, which pays 85 per cent of insurance costs for employees and retirees, switched to a lower rate company. The second invoice referred to a visit to Dr. McNulty's office: $90 for the office visit and $110 for x-rays, with a medicare payment of $82.75 and $35.81, and the usual $0 from Blue Cross. (After contacting the school representative regarding the "This particular service is not covered under your contract.", I was informed that the contract does not cover office visits.)

After the month of very dry weather—good for golf and working in the yard, but bad for plants and gardens—we have had two straight weeks of wind and rain and some violent thunderstorms. At least when it was dry one could water whatever needed it; but there is no way to turn off the rain and accompaning plant drowning and soil erosion.

My golf game has been lousy so far with one exception. My team won second place in the opening scramble on May 20th with a gross of 69. Practically everything went right that day. But in the daily play, and especially with the Dillies, the chipping and putting have been lousy. I have had four rounds in the 90's and the rest in the 80's. My lowest score is 83, and my handicap is up to 13.

The external beam radiation treatment for 38 days was completed on Thursday, July 26, 2001. A checkup with Dr. Gebara, Radiation Oncologist, is scheduled for August 24th. That will be mainly to ask how I am doing and feeling. This week I can go back to eating lots of salads, fruits and vegetables and high fiber foods. They were curtailed during treatment as diahrrea frequently occurs as a result of the affect on the bowels.

Thursday afternoon, I produced a video on prostate cancer at the Radiation Oncology Center at BMC with Rosemary Crawford and Richard Coleman on cameras. Dr. Gebara and two radiation Therapists had agreed to participate, feeling that the more information the public receives, especially aging males, the better chance of early detection and treatment. One disturbing fact during the interview was the statement by Dr. Gebara that studies have shown that patients who have undergone treatment and those who have not generally have about the same life expectancy since prostate cancer is usually a slow growing one and most people die of other factors. The basic difference is in the quality of life.

The 33rd Family Reunion was held at Bucksteep Manor in the Bershires on Saturday, July 28, with Richard Brinson as host. There were 22 people in attendance and 16 who stayed for dinner. Following the meal, we held a discussion and vote on several factors including everyone over 18 paying $25, how often to hold reunions, a designated member of each family to collect dues and forward to treasurer, publish list of those paid, and check for next rotation. An e-mail was sent to family members and also posted on the family Web site requesting an immediate response. Thus far, four days later, only one person has replied. So I think it is safe to assume that those not in attendance and not responding have no interest in maintaining the family reunion tradition, and we older members will have to be content with getting our families together several times per year, as we have done this past year. Many younger people have their own interests and priorities, and we have to accept that fact.

Two PSA tests have been done since my radiation treatment and both registered 0.5, which usually means that the cancer cells have been destroyed. The hormone shots have been discontinued but it will be some time before the hot flashes cease, although they have diminished somewhat in intensity. Erectile disfunction will probably be permanent as the radiation treatment zapped the nerve bundles beside the prostate which stimulate erection. Also some permanent damage was done to the bladder and uretha as the burning sensation on urination continues with a weak stream and frequent trips to the bathroom day and night.

The leader of the Prostate Cancer Support Group is spending the winter traveling about the country with his wife in their mobile home, and has asked me to serve as facilitator for November and December. Rosemary and I videotaped the December presentation by a Dr. from Albany and the entire program will be shown on Dalton Community TV. I also taped an interview at the Oncology—Hematology Center, on Conte

Drive near the Archives, pertaining to a Prostate cancer prevention trial which is enlisting some 30,000 volunteers across the country to test the viability of using Selenium and Vitamin E for prevention. (A few years later it was determined that the process was not effective.)

Orthoscopic surgery on my left leg was scheduled for November 30th, after I had completed the outdoor chores relating to the tool shed, flower bed cleanup, and mulching; and had removed the two layers of tile in the kitchen and laid down a parquet floor. Family members had come for the weekend before Thanksgiving and helped with cleaning the cellar and the outdoor chores, including an overhead cover for the space between the garage side door and the house entrance. Eleanor helped with the roof project and also did most of the installation of a new door that had a different side opening to the sunroom. The surgery went well and with a spinal anesthesia, I was able to watch part of the procedure on the monitor as the probe glided through the two holes made adjacent to the knee, slicing off tissue. This non invasive procedure is scheduled as day surgery and a few hours later I was back home. I had a prescription for a pain killer and took a couple of them that afternoon and night. They were monstrous and I had difficulty swallowing them. Breaking them in half did not improve matters much. After resting that day and all night, I wanted some activity the following moming. So I went to the studio, to the Mall to get a flu shot, and to the store for a few items. The leg was stlll heavily bandaged but walking was not painful nor too difficult. I only used the cane they gave me for my trip to the car and home, and gave it to Rosemary. I was given a series of exercises to do daily to prevent excessive swelling and to assist healing. These are usually done around 5 a.m. while laying in bed before arising. The arm exercises for my torn rotator cuff are also done at that time using a wand. Several weeks later there is more discomfort than following the surgery. Of course, going up and down stairs to clean the cellar, out in the wood room, and up and down the ladder to work on the cover between doors has not been too kind to the leg. Today, at the Mall, I decided to do a walk around the perimeter so I will probably keep my provisional appointment with the Orthopaedic surgeon, Dr. Cella, scheduled for January 11, 2002. Also this lends support to my decision to forego the surgery on the shoulder. That would mean some serious cutting and stiching and months to heal with no gaurantee that things would improve.

Rosemary and I have finally been relieved of the responsibility of running the Forever Young group at church. After several special meetings and discussions, we were able to get a committee together to take charge.

The name was changed briefly to FBC Social Club as suggested by the ministers, but that didn't fly and was withdrawn. The age level was reduced to 55 and later removed. Any adults in the church are welcome to attend the dinners and programs which are held on the second Sunday in the month, with the exception of May, when it is held the third Sunday in order not to conflict with Mother's Day. We will continue to prepare the meals for the time being, usually alternating each month so that one of us can attend the meeting. Ruth is now the Treasurer.

It is readily apparent that I have spent an inordinate amount of time during the past year discussing health problems. This probably can be attributed to a record number of mishaps and physical woes happening to a person who has led a very active physical and mental life, and who has considerable difficulty dealing with the frustrations of restricted activity. In the future greater emphasis will be placed on family life.

Volunteers at the Silvio Conte National Archives will have an opportunity next week to do some advanced previewing of the 1930 Census records. Wednesday, February 27, 2002, A government official will be there at 2 p.m. to conduct a swearing in. We have to swear that we will not divulge any information obtained in the family searches prior to the official release on April 1st. Friday, Connie Potters, a woman from the Washington office who has spent the last eight years working on the 1930 Census, will be there for a pot luck supper and to lecture us on procedures for obtaining data. Saturday from 9 a.m. to 3 p.m. will be our research opportunity. This will better equip us to deal with the expected onslaught of visitors starting the first of April. And that night, the editor of our Newsletter, Archival Anecdotes, will be hosting a fireside buffet dinner at her home in Tyringham for the guest speaker and board members.

Our septic system had not been cleaned out for about 15 years and we thought it was still fine because at that time it was only about half full.
Late Sunday afternoon, I happened to be walking in the hallway by the cellar steps when I heard the sound of running water hitting the floor downstairs as Rosemary flushed the toilet. The water to the toilet was shut off and we spent a great deal of time moving the items that had been stacked in that spot under the plumbing pipes by our family when the playroom was made more accessible, and mopping up the water. A message was left for the plumber and I called again Monday morning. He came out around noon and checked the outflow from both toilets, the bathtub and the kitchen sink, and said the line from the house to the septic tank seemed to be plugged. He didn't have the equipment to deal

with that and suggested that I call someone in the septic cleaning business. The first call got an answering machine. The second one reached JSSJR Enterprises, Inc. Berkshire Septic, located in Lanesboro who sent out two men that afternoon. After removing the plug on the house end of the outlet line and letting the backed up water flow out, they confirmed that the line was clogged. They went outside to dig for the cover and after two diggings of 2 ft. holes, found the opening. I was called over to view the blockage—mainly toilet paper. It was cleaned out, but the level of the tank was only a few inches below the pipe. He said the tank needed emptying and a chimney should be built to a few inches below the surface for easier access in the future. I said the next time was probably something for my heirs to worry about. He said they would be extremely grateful. I authorized the recommended service and the next morning a tank cleaning truck, a backhoe tractor and their service truck all came out to do the job and presented me with the bill for a little over $1,000.

There was still water leaking through the floor around the toilet so we had to have the plumber come the next morning to replace the wax sealing at the base. Hopefully, our problems are over for a very long time. But it is probably a lot like cars: each time there is a different problem.

Today, I took my completed interview with Don Kirkpatrick to his house for review and corrections or amendments. While there I asked him if he was going to be sworn in to participate in the 1930 census preview for volunteers. To my utter amazement and chagrin, he said the swearing in took place on the 20th. I had marked my calendar for the 27th. I went out to the Archives and talked to Jean Nudd and she said she was sorry that I missed it and that I could not participate in the workshop. Arriving home, I sent an e-mail to Arthur Dukakis, director of the Northeast Region, bureau of the Census, who did the swearing in, and asked if I could drive to Boston for the swearing in to take place any time before Tuesday. No response has been received as yet.

On Monday morning, when I had not received any response from Arthur Dukakis regarding my swearing in, I called his office and reiterated my situation. He said he had made the same mistake about calendar entries; and said he didn't want me to drive to Boston and back, and he could not come out here, but he would try to arrange for someone from the Albany office to come to the Berkshires. Tuesday I received a call from Mary Ann Von Wagner of the Springfield office stating that Mr. Dukakis had instructed her to come to the Archives and swear me in. We set a time of 10:30 a.m. on Wednesday. That was also the day I had agreed to do the soup and sandwich luncheon for FBC's Lenten series from 12 to

1, and had bowling at 1, so I made the Vegetable soup on Tuesday and prepared the Tuna salad sandwiches Wednesday morning, placed them in the refrigerator at church and put the soup on low heat to warm up, before going to the Archives. Mrs. Wagner was about 40 minutes late, but finally showed up and swore me in. She said she had called my house to say she would be late, but I had already gone. I had to leave immediately, but Betty Quadrozzi, President of the Friends was there and offered to give her a tour of the premises.

So I will be able to attend the work session on Saturday from 9-3 to search the 1930 census.

Saturday was one of the best days I have ever spent at the Archives, and I was there for the full six hours, from 9 a.m. to 3 p.m. I found out how to check for ED numbers, sheet and line numbers and the roll of microfilm to peruse, and found my family living in Mobile County in 1930 with four children, along with grandparents, Frank and Emma Wright, with Edward and Irma still at home, and Ernest and Rose Wright with five of their children. Ernest and his family were listed as part of Frank's household.

There were some mistakes: Crawford was spelled Crofford, Ruth was listed as Mary R. and Daddy's parents were listed as both being born in Illinois. Also Frank's mother was listed as being born in Alabama. Frank's property was valued at $2000 and ours at $1000.

After lunch I looked up the search material for Normal, Illinois and will check out the Crawfords in that area on my next visit. It was decided that we volunteers needed more practice and experience in using all the material available on the computer, soundexes, catalogues, and microfilm in order to better assist the avalanche of researchers expected to descend upon us starting the first of April. Therefore, we will be allowed to work on the Census every Saturday until the first.

There was a shocking experience on Saturday, March 16, 2002 at the V.F.W. Hall on Linden Street where the Berkshire Chapter of the American Culinary Federation (ACF) was hosting its 14th Annual Gourmet dinner-Dance as a fund raiser for our scholarship fund. I was busy videotaping the affair as I usually do, when, after dinner, Jim Guiden, former president and current secretary, announced that they were going to present the Chapter Chef of the Year Award. As he began to read some of the information, I thought "Hey, that's me he is talking about." Most of the information came from a booklet that had been prepared for Senior member recognition at a luncheon during the Northeast Regional Conference in Cleveland a couple of years ago. It contained information about work experiences, education, hobbies, etc. that I had submitted. I had to stop taping and go up front and receive the Award. Another chef took the camera and filmed the event. I received a long necklace ribbon with the words "Chef of the Year" on it and a medal at the end with the seal of the ACF and the same words on it. The camera was laid down while I accepted handshakes and congratulations. Unfortunately, in the excitement, the camera was still recording but was not focused on anything in particular, so I lost a considerable amount of useful footage, including recognition of the people involved in preparing and serving the dinner.

On Wednesday, March 13th, I went to Simon's Rock College in Great Barrington and recorded a W.E.B. DuBois memorial lecture by Dr. Manning Marable, professor of History and Political Science at Columbia University in New York City, and founding Director of the Institute for Research African American Studies. The entire program was very interesting and informative. With a question and answer period after the lecture, the program was about an hour and a half. Refreshments followed downstairs where people could engage in further discussion and autographs.

During the past week, thanks to the rush not materializing at the Archives, I was able to locate and make copies of pages of the 1930 census containing the Crawfords in Illinois and the Persips in Pittsfield.

The Normal/Bloomington one mainly confirmed the information I already had. with additional responses about value of house if owned, literacy, radio, occupation and place of employment. This Morning, Friday, Ruth met me at the Archives to look up the Evans family in Pittsfield and make a copy of the sheet.

I was called by Jean Nudd, the Archivist in charge, last night with a request to come in tonight from 5 or 6 to 9 p.m. to assist people as they are short of volunteers for that time period.

Tomorrow I will spend all day at Pathfinder School in Palmer where the Master gardeners are conducting a symposium with workshop classes on several dozen garden topics. There will also be soil testing and tables with answers to questions during the break and lunch. I am scheduled to man a table about wildlife as a hazard to gardens.

And on Sunday the Berkshire Baptist Association will have its annual meeting in Westfield in conjunction with the Pioneer Valley Association.

After the 4 p.m. meetings a dinner will be served followed by a musical program at 7 p.m.

The 33rd Crawford Family reunion was held in Wallingford, PA at the home of J. Alvin stout, 111 on July 27, 2002. Rooms had been reserved by Isaac A. at the Ramada Inn on Route 95 near the Airport for up to ten family groups. I think there were 7 rooms used. Rosemary and I and our great grand children, Joshua and Ashley departed Dalton in mid-morning on July 26 for the approximately 6 hour drive to PA. Unfortunately, we followed the New Jersey Turnpike all the way to Delaware and had to go up 95 North for about 30 miles. We also had made a mistake in thinking that 284 south off of the NY Throughway would lead us to the NJ Turnpike at a point further South than going down the Garden State Parkway. After many miles, we checked at a stop in a small town and were told that we had to take a road East to the Garden State and follow it south to the turnpike. This also increased our travel distance and time. We arrived around 6 p.m. at the Ramada, checked in, and ate the rest of the sandwiches we had packed in a cooler along with fruit, soda and tea.

Philip Crawford was the only early arrival with his wife, Anita. Checking in later were Peter and Helen with their daughter, Cheryl and husband, Frank Nelson and daughters, Tiffany and Chantel; Ruth and Daughters, Karen and Pamela Rouse with husband George and son, Matthew. Arriving around midnight were Rosemary and Vernell Smith and son, Richard.

We communicated by phones and visits to rooms and met in the dining room for breakfast and in the lobby for car pooling to Alvin's house around 11:30 Saturdy morning. Richard and Margaret Brinson stayed at another hotel.

Alvin has a large beautiful house in Wallingford. A prosecuter for the Justice Department in Philadelphia for many years, he moved to this site a couple of years ago. About 50 members, friends and relatives of the Stouts came during the afternoon and created quite a crowd along with the Crawford family. Horseshoes and badminton were popular games outside while many of the children played a variety of games in the basement family room where a catered buffet was set up for dinner in the early evening. For lunch a picnic setting was available with grilled franks and hamburgers, baked beans and salads, beer and sodas.

Marie and Alvin were brought from the Veterans Hospital by daughters Linda Ford and Jacqueline and warmly greeted by all in attendance.

After dinner a talent show was held with rap singing, piano playing, poetry and a violin solo.

I gave Alvin copies of the census records of his father and grandfather that I had looked up at the Archives for 1920 and 1930.

There was a lot of chit-chat between various groups but no formal family meeting or discussion was held.

Pam and Karen will host next year's reunion.

My new digital video camera and tripod were taken to the reunion and many scenes were recorded. Also, on Sunday, as we checked out and departed for home, we stopped in Philadelphia for a tour of the visitor's Center, the Liberty Bell and Independence Hall. These were all captured on video and will be part of my TV show.

My golf game has finally shown some signs of life. At the Senior tournament held at Waubeeka in Williamstown on Monday, I shot an 88 and won first low net in my division. The 88 could have been much better except for a couple of unbelievable errors. I had 2 triple bogies resulting from popping the balls into a pond and the river due to lousy shots. But I did have 7 pars and 1 bird. The 88 isn't a great score, but it is ten strokes better than I did at Taconic last month for my worst round ever, 98.

The very next day with the Dillies, I had 10 pars and a gross of 83, my lowest score of the year. Here again I topped a drive into the pond in front of the tee on the par three 13th hole at Wahconah for a triple bogey 6. Consistency is still a problem, but hopefully, with two days of improved golf, the string of bogies and double bogies is diminishing for good this season.

During the winter of 02-03, we scheduled a trip to San Jose in January using my accumulated frequent flier mileage. Unfortunately, when scheduling the date, I had forgotten the annual meeting at First Baptist Church on January 26th, which would be my last task as Moderator as I had opted to resign after almost seven years. (Presiding at all church meetings was an easy task, but serving on the Board of Trustees was becoming more frustrating and time consuming as they haggled over the budget and other issues at frequent 3 hour meetings) It cost me $200 to reschedule the flight for Frebruary 13 with a return on March 3. Ruth accompanied us on the trip and we enjoyed our stay in the new home of Gwen, Isaac Allen and Jillion.

The 35th Family Reunion was hosted by Ruth Crawford Evans' family led by Karen in Hartford, CT, on July 26, 2003. The Picnic was held at the Williams Pavilion at Whickham Park and attended by the following family groups: Stouts, 7; Peter Crawfords, 5; Isaac Crawfords, 6; Ruth C. Evans, 6. The park is very large and has dozens of areas available for group picnicing. A large trailer was parked nearby and offered free blood pressure screening to all of those interested. Many of us participated.

A lovely buffet dinner was served at George's Restaurant and a lot of family dialogue ensued along with many photo options. Again, however, no formal business meeting was held to plan for the future or to rehash old issues.

It is my family's turn for the 36th Reunion and it has been decided to host it here at the house in Dalton. Rosemary C. Smith and Isaac Allen will make most of the plans and arrangements. a list of accommodations has been published on the Family web site along with the advice to make reservations early as Summer is a very busy tourist time in the Berkshires. I was asked to make arrangements for the Dinner and met with the Caterer for the VFW in Dalton to discuss the buffet menu and signed a contract with a deposit for Saturday, July 24th. Eric will secure a tent for the back yard for the picnic.

Horseshoes and badminton will be available along with other entertainment planned by Isaac and Rosemary. As of March 21, there has been only one response on the Family web site, and that was a maybe.

Four of us will be flying to San Jose in late May for Jill's graduation on the 29th from Archbishop Mitty High School. Jill is a straight A student and has applied to several colleges for enrollment and scholarships. She has been offered a full four year scholarship at Northeastern University in Boston and Scholarship assistance at the University of Southern California. Because of the hazardous winters in the Northeast area, she is giving serious consideration to schools in California.

Isaac A. has taken a new position with Macy's at its exclusive store in Palo Alto adjacent to Stanford U and near Gwen's Stationary store, "Letter Perfect". He is desperate to increase his income after the past few years of part time consulting and jobs.

Rosemary C. Smith is currently working two jobs; her old one and a night time job 4 days per week at the office of Elder Service.

Vanessa has moved out and is living with a girl friend. Her high school graduation is in limbo as she has failed a couple of classes.

I have finally joined the new generation update by purchasing a cell phone. Doing a lot of driving alone, it seemed logical to have some recourse in case of emergency. Also with only one line at home, it is frequently impossible to make a necessary phone call if my wife is on line on the computer or talking on the phone for a long time. She makes the same complaint but at least she had a cell phone for calls when the line was in use thanks to our daughter's gift. One of the frustrations of old age is the difficulty in understanding and adapting to new devices and techniques. Hopefully, I will eventually acquire the ability to input all of the necessary information. I purchased a Verizon Motorola folding phone with battery chargers for in house and in the car, a leather case, and a headset for avoiding the use of the hands on the phone when driving. The purchase was made at the Verizon store on Riverdale Road in W. Springfield. I stopped there while on my way to the home and garden show at Eastern States Exposition complex. There is a $39.99 monthly fee for unlimited use of the cell phone, plus my standard $41 monthly charge for regular phone. Add another $22 for internet connection and I will be paying over $100 per month for wire and wireless hookups, plus $52 monthly for sattelite dish hookup.

The economy of the past three years under the administration of George W. Bush continues its decline while the cost of living continues its upward sweep. Huge tax cuts have been granted to the wealthy. Interest rates are lower than they have been in fifty years, which may be great for home and auto buyers; but for seniors on fixed income with savings and CD accounts, it has been devastating. While we hang on to the stocks we have in hopes that the market will recover, there is certainly little desire to invest in new funds for long time growth at our ages. Gasoline and fuel oil costs have reached an all time high due to the cut back in production in order to rev up prices. Many large production corporations continue to escalate the movement of manufacturing to third world countries with lower pay scales, causing a hugh increase in the unemployment rate in the good old USA.

The war in Iraq was based on false premises that Saddam Hussein had weapons of mass destruction and was linked to Al Qaida, the instigator of the 9/11 attack on the Trade Center and the Pentagon through its leader, Osama Bin Laden. It turns out that this war was part of the Bush plan from the beginning in an effort to complete the job that his father started as President in the early 90's. But the Iraquis were smart. Troops surrendered and were allowed to return to civilian life, where many of them have resorted to sneaky attacks with mortar, rockets and bombs to slaughter over 500 Americans plus many civilians and people from other countries.

The so called rebuilding of the country was awarded to corporate supporters of the Republican administration with overcharges on many items. A new democratic form of government is supposed to be formed by June of 20004, but with rivalries between ethnic and religious groups it is doubtful if that effort will be successful. Bush now wants to get the troops out by Summer in order to focus on the impending politcal battle for the presidency against Democratic rival, John Kerry, Senator from Massachusetts. It will be an interesting battle. Hopefully, there will be an honest vote counting and election this time with none of the shennanigans of the 2000 one, which put Bush in office with the help of the Supreme Court.

It is also suspected that Bush will now make a great effort to capture or kill Bin Laden before the election in order to enhance his chances for victory. This will also help to take some of the focus off the domestic problems he has created with massive tax cuts for the wealthy, environmental destruction, and medicare and prescription drug cost escalation.

As of this date, March 30, 2004, it looks like the Family Reunion here in Dalton may be a disaster. Still no sign ups, and a posting on the family web site by Rosemary revealed that most rooms in the area have already been booked for that weekend. I sent emails to members of the Brinson family, Vernita's offspring, and sibling, inviting them to get involved for a change. None have responded as yet.

Ruth said Peter has made reservations at a motel in Dalton, so his family will be represented. Linda, of the Stout family, said it would be about a month before she knew definitely if she and her significant other would be able to attend.

For Jill's graduation, Isaac A. says there are about 18 members of the Gasque and Crawford families planning to attend, and all expecting to stay with them. That would be impossible; so he is considering contacting motels to see if a special room rate could be obtained. On Saturday, after the graduation, we will all eat at some food establishment and on Sunday the family will feed all of us at his house.

My wife, Eric and I flew from Albany to Washington, DC and then to San Jose on United Airlines for The Memorial Day weekend and Jill's graduation. Rosemary departed from Manchester, NH for the trip and we arrived about the same time on Thursday evening. Accomodations at the hotel were nice but the $400 plus bill was not something that I was expecting. It was nice to see many of the Gasques whom we hadn't seen in years and share memories and comaradie.

Friday evening activities for the 300 plus graduating class were held outdoors in a courtyard with much music and celebration. The Graduation ceremony was held in the stadium on Saturday morning with families and guests seated in the grandstand and in chairs on the field. Naturally, I had my digital video camera and took much footage of events over the weekend and especially Jill approaching the stage to receive her diploma and many shots of family members at the reception at the hotel and meals at Isaac's place.

Jill has decided to go to the University of Southern California (USC) in Los Angeles and will be starting in Mid August.

Back home, the hectic events of summer began. We had too many projects in the works to successfully complete them all in time for the reunion. I had taken down the rusty rabbit fence with several strands of barbed wire above it to keep the deer out of my vegetable garden. The 12 raised beds were shifted a few feet to the right to make more room for driving down to the area where the tent would would be set up for the family reunion picnic and to the start of the pond where I was working on a new inlet. I put up new poles anchored in cement for the 6 ft green vinyl coated wire fence and installed a gate for entry. The concrete for the poles, for the rebuilding of the back steps, and for making a new pipe line water entrance from the brook was all done by mixing with a shovel in the wheelbarrow. Needless to say, picking up and handling over 40 bags of concrete mix and shoveling it into place reeked havoc on my hands and back; but we got the job done.

Meanwhile, Rosemary started sorting stuff out in the cellar for disposal and had Joshua assist her. Since we don't work too well together, (there can't be two bosses), this was a good arrangement. I only got involved in moving heavy equipment and disposing of the throw aways.

She had another major task that came up. Her brother, Alfred, had a diabetic problem. His blood sugar was jumping up and down with his forgetting to take his insulin, and after several hospital visits it was decided that he would move from his apartment to a care facility. She has held a power of attorney to take care of his finances and other events for a few years now and decided that it would require about a month to clean out all of his posessions including thousands of video tapes. Unfortunately, many of his things ended up in our cellar negating the positive effects of the cleanup. We did have room however for family members to sleep for the reunion in July as this transfer took place in August.

Another major calamity occurred the weekend of July 4th. I made arrangements to rent a large bulldozer from a tractor company in order to dredge several years accumulation of silt from the pond. In the past, smaller ones with wheels had occasionally gotten stuck in the quicksand like mud. This one had a caterpillar tread like an army tank and with its weight could compact the muck to the rock bed underneath. It was delivered on Friday, and although I had paid for two days use it would not be picked up until Tuesday Morning. Friday afternoon I decided to try it out and drove slowly into the water over a spot that I have used for an entry for about 25 years. I began pushing the silt to the south wall of the pond with success and believed that everything was going to work out. After two hours, I came out for a break and then went back in for another two hours. This time as I came out, I heard a roaring sound and looked back to see a geyser shooting about 30 feet into the air. There is a 14 inch water main which runs across the back yard underground and through the pond under the dam and across the brook on the western end of the yard. Although there were several feet of earth over the entry way, apparently the weight of the monstrous dozer was too much for the 150 year old pipeline causing a rupture. The Dalton Water commissioner was called and came out with a crew to survey the damage. When I explained what had happened, he said, "We can't say it was an act of God. You are responsible". For several hours they stood around while the pond became half filled with water. Then they finally had the water shut off and brought in 3 pumps to remove the water for another several hours. After midnight they excavated the site around the pipeline and began removal and replacement of a ten foot section. I was billed for the hours of labor, use of equipment, parts, and gallons of water for the 20 families affected while the system was checked for contamination for several days. The total charge was a little over $4000. Fortunately, this liability was covered by my homeowners insurance. I had to supply pictures of the disaster and a copy of the invoice from the Water District.

A crew from the Dalton Conservation District came out about a week later and informed me that in the future I had to obtain a permit to do any dredging of the pond and would have to build a new entrance away from the water line. The Commissioner said I had done a great job in improving the property; but despite it being private property and approval for building the pond about 30 years ago, I still had to follow the current rules, as it also affected my neighbors. I received a packet of information and documents regarding permit approval for any future dredging. So it looks like the area will eventually revert to the swamp it was when I started the landscaping.

The 36th Crawford Family Reunion took place here on Saturday, July 24, 2004 with about 28 people in attendance, mainly from the families of

Peter, Ruth and Isaac. Donald and Joyce Stout were the only members of Marie's family present. Eric provided a small tent and we borrowed tables and chairs from First Baptist Church for the picnic. Luckily, the weather was ideal: sunny and warm. Despite the burning candle poles and having sprayed the area that morning, some mosquitoes were present and annoying to some guests. Rosemary C. Smith and Isaac A. were the planners for the occasion with Rosemary supplying most of the food and beverage. We enjoyed the food, horseshoes, baloon tossing as staged by Isaac Allen and card playing. Dinner that night was catered at the VFW hall in Dalton, where we showed a video of me singing a couple of songs, Peter said Grace, and we enjoyed a buffet meal. After dinner Isaac played Jeopardy using family genealogy data for questions. The evening concluded with picture taking, and my inviting everyone to come to the house for brunch the following morning.

Scheduled to sing a solo at First Baptist Church on my birthday, June 25, 2006, I shared a list of songs with the new organist, Christina Guerra, now Christina Oberfield. These were songs that I had sung in previous years. She suggested "His Eye is on the Sparrow", which I had done only once a few years ago. She was familiar with the music and I remembered the words, so we ran through it briefly after church. A full rehearsal was scheduled for Friday night. I ran through the music several times at home and made a copy for her. I played in the Senior golf tournament at Wyantenuck Country Club on Monday afternoon and ate the buffet dinner that followed. By Tuesday afternoon after playing only 2 holes of golf in the rain with the Dillies, I began to feel more discomfort. My eyes and nose were running and I was beginning some throat problems. Things got worse over the next several days, and I began to wonder if I should notify people at church that someone else should fill in. My biggest fear was that in the middle of the song I would choke up and lose my voice. That would be a disastrous embarrassment for me and would spoil the spiritual continuity of the service. I went to church Friday night and had to wait about 40 minutes as a wedding rehearsal was taking place with the organist supplying the music. When we ran through the song, I sang softly trying to avoid excessive strain on my vocal cords. But after a couple of runs I started to cough and gag. I explained my problem to her and she suggested singing in a lower key to make things easier. I still had hopes that things would improve by Sunday and did not cancel. On Saturday night while lying in bed, I prayed to God that I would make it through the number on Sunday; not for my ego, but in praise of him and for the spiritual enrichment of the congregation. Sunday, I arrived at 9:15 A M and we rehearsed the number a couple of times. Several people wished me luck and one gave me a small sucker to help my throat. I did not sing any of the hymns during the service nor did I read the parts of the script for the congregation. After the sermon, The pastor, Bob Rennie, looked at me and nodded, indicating that it was time to step forward and sing. I went up to the lectern, looked at the organist and she began the intro. With some trepidation, I began. Singing two verses and the refrain, I got stronger as the song progressed and heard a chorus of Amens when I finished. During the friendly hour in the Assembly Hall after the service many people came over, shook my hand or hugged me and said how great I sounded. One woman said I had never sounded better, and one gentleman said he was in tears as I sang. The organist went over to the piano and played "Happy Birthday" while people sang. It was overwhelming. Surely God answered my prayer. The next day I went to do my weekly hour plus reading for the Blind and Dyslexic and got hoarse and choked up several times; further evidence that a miracle occurred on Sunday.

Serving on two committees for TABCOM has made a lot of travel necessary: The Search Committee for a new Executive Minister and the Personnel Committee. Personnel isn't so bad, But the Search one consumes a great deal of time and effort. Both groups meet at the First Baptist Church in Worcester which is 200 plus miles away roundtrip and a two hour trip both ways for a two hour meeting. We had about 30 applications each containing resumes and other information. The list was narrowed to 14 and five questions were submitted for their response. At our last meeting we reduced the list to seven and requested a video response to additional questions. At our next meeting in December three finalists will be selected and will be interviewed in February at Andover Newton Seminary where one of our committee members is employed. Hopefully, after that day's sessions we will be able to pick the new Director for TABCOM.

Four finalists were actually chosen to be interviewed at our February 11th session at Andover Newton, and by nighttime a final decision was made for the new Executive Minister: Tony Pappas, who is currently Area Minister for the Old Colony Association right here in TABCOM.

This Search Committee was an expensive proposition for TABCOM. Not for the members who volunteered their time and effort, but for the costs of all the paperwork, travel arrangements and hotel rooms for 3 of the candidates. One was a Missionary in Belgium, another a minister in California. The third one came from Schenectady, NY, which isn't too far away.

I have never served on a Committee with such divergent and obsessive viewpoints and opinions. But we finally got the job done, and now it is up to the Board of Directors to give final approval at their March meeting and submit the information to the churches for their approval.

In October, I purchased a 2004 Doge Neon for my wife to replace her 1991 Dodge Spirit. I also purchased a John Deere Tractor last fall to replace my 35 year old International Harvester one. And this winter I bought a small portable greenhouse on E-Bay from a Connecticut company. I will have to wait until Spring to put it together behind the garage when the snow and ice have departed.

Well George W. Bush pulled it off again. He won the reelection with a narrow victory in Ohio. Although there wasn't as much controversy as occurred In Florida in 2000, there were long delays at strategic polling places, especially in poor neighborhoods. John Kerry conceded the next morning without challenging the outcome, which disappointed many of his constituents. Bush carried the revamped South which has largely deserted the Democratic Party in favor of the far right conservative and, so called, religious and moral values of the current Republican Party. How gullible can people really be to swallow the Bush Lies, deception and hypocracy about such issues as medicare, Social Security, No Child Left Behind, tax cuts, weapons of mass destruction and the budget. Plus the continued deaths of American military personnel and many Iraquis after the victory was declared in a publicity stunt on an aircraft carrier. Also the corporate welfare he continues to provide for big business. Its beyond comprehension.
On the other hand, Kerry could have been a little more forceful in his attacks on the Bush administration and not concede so readily. Perhaps he wished to remain in the Senate and watch the collapse of the Republican Party and the economy under Bush's second term.

I have been doing a digitally recorded reading at the Recording for the Blind & Dyslexic Studio in Lenox for the past few years on Wednesdays at 4 p m. before switching to Monday. Books read are in response to requests from all over the country sent to headquarters in Princeton, NJ and cover a wide variety of subjects. I have read a wide variety of topics such as History, Geography, Medicine, Science, Religion, Sociology, Psychology, Art, Biographies, and Essays. Some are boring,some very enlightening, and some highly emotional. Last week was the first time that I became completely overwhelmed and had to stop for a few minutes. I was reading two essays by Martin Luther King: "Letter From a Birmingham Jail" written during his incarceration in that city on trumped up charges of civil disobedience; and his "I Have a Dream" speech during the March On Washington in the 60's. I had read the Birmingham letter many years ago when it was printed in the local newspaper but had only read and heard excerpts in newspapers and on radio and TV of the Washington speech on Martin Luther King Day. As I uttered the words aloud and connected with the times and conditions of that period, my voice began to quiver and tears welled in my eyes. The lady who was monitoring the reading and recording said, "Why don't you take a break". I looked up to see her eyes running also. So I took a walk, got a drink of water, wiped my eyes and cleared my throat several times before completing the essay. I agreed with her that the words were very moving and had a tremendous impact. That speech was probably instrumental in identifying Dr. King as a national hero.

Five years after the orthoscopic surgery to cut away the cartilidge on my knee I had developed considerable pain from the resulting bone on bone that required total knee replacement. Surgery was scheduled for September 2007. For several months following replacement, the leg remained swollen off and on. An ultrasound review of the leg veins revealed no clots or blockage, but I think that problem along with developing higher blood pressure and cholesterol levels contributed to my problem in December. On Christmas Eve, about 3 p.m., I began to feel pressure under my sternum and relaxed in a reclining chair for a couple of hours before dinner with no change in the discomfort. at 10 p.m. we went to church for choir rehearsal before the 11p.m. candlelight service and communion. I sang without any changes in feelings and served communion before returning home at 12:30. Going to bed after 1, I spent 2 hours lying there with the pressure continuing and about 3 a.m. decided that a visit to the emergency room was warranted. Waking up my wife, Rosemary, and son, Isaac Allen, who came home that morning for a visit from California, they took me to the Berkshire Medical Center. While Rosemary went to park, Isaac rushed in and told them at the desk about my condition. They rushed out with a wheel chair and took me in for a series of questions, tests and medications over several hours. with no positive diagnosis or results. They decided to keep me overnight for observation and 6 hours after my arrival, finally took me upstairs for a room. About 10 o'clock in the morning, Dr. Fribush, who was substituting for my primary care physician came in, asked a few questions, looked at the reports, checked me out and said he would be back shortly. He made arrangements for me to be flown by helicopter to Albany Medical Center for catherization and angioplasty, (procedures that BMC does not do and patients are either sent to Albany or Bay State Hospital in Springfield). I called home and told them what was going on before my 11 minute flight to the medical center. The procedure revealed about 80% blockage in one of my arteries. A baloon on a tube inserted through the groin area compressed the platelets on the artery wall and a wire stint was inserted to increase blood flow. Medications were given for high levels of blood pressure and cholesterol and I was able to have dinner a few hours later. Family communicated with the nurses and Dr. Brady, and told him whatever they wanted about my activities and stubborness. The next day I was allowed to get up and walk around and was told that I would probably go home the following day. Eric drove over with them in his van because they thought that would be a better ride than sitting in a low small car. I was given 6 prescriptions and a small vial of nitroglycerin tablets to take for a time, and told not to drive, lift anything heavy or do any strenuous activity for 2 weeks until I saw Dr. Brady again. These instructions were followed to the letter, and things were going great for about 10 days when the same pain started again at suppertime. I took a nitro under my tongue with no change, took another with the same lack of results and decided to go to the hospital. This visit resulted in a five hour delay for a room and a series of the same old tests over and over again for 2 days before being sent home. The pain this time had only lasted about an hour. I walked around the wing several times and watched a lot of tv. Dr. McNulty came in and looked at the test results including a drug induced cardiac stress test and said I could go home. Instead of a wheel chair I was told I could walk to the elevator and to the car as my heart was as strong as a much younger person. My visit with Dr. Brady who has an office in Pittsfield and comes over on Wednesdays was positive. I asked about the persistent cough I continued to experience. He said he knew which medication caused it and had been planning to increase the dosage. Instead he changed to another drug and the cough has greatly diminished. Rosemary asked him about going back to the hospital again if I got more chest pain. she was finally realizing that what I had said about it being a fund raiser, keeping you several days and performing the same xrays, scans, ekg's, etc. was a torture chamber which only increased the stress and discomfort, especially pulling the hairs off your chest several times per day. Dr. Brady said he wouldn't go back. Just keep taking the medication. So now I drive, do simple tasks around the house, exercise, try to eat sensibly and have had no more problems. I went bowling on Thursday with the Dillies and had my best series of the season. I will substitute in the Senior league on Wednesdays but will not bowl 3 days consecutively as I had been doing for years.

Another problem that probably contributed to my earlier stress was my susceptability to fraud by a car dealership that supposedly was offering gifts during a 3 day car sale in Great Barrington. Taking my "winning" ticket numbers down, I was informed that I did not win the new car listed. And another prize was a Walmart gift certificate ranging from $5 to $5,000. Naturally just about everyone had the $5 one. The whole purpose was to immediately have a salesperson take you outside to check out all the cars with baloons on them that were for sale. Since my salesman was black, I decided to take a look. After showing me several cars with no appeal, I looked at a Pontiac G6 that had been on lease for the past year. It was an 07 model. My 1998 Plymouth Voyager van was 10 years old and still performing well and was expected to be my last car, but I agreed to go for a spin in the Pontiac. While sitting so low was not especially desirable, all of the power features were, and I agreed to discuss the sales features. We came to an agreement on the sales price and the value of my exchange vehicle, and he went for a discussion with the sales manager and said the manager would be ready for me soon. I told the Salesman that I had a luncheon meeting in Pittsfield at noon and it was starting to snow heavily at 10 a.m. I should have departed then instead of sitting around for over an hour waiting. I had asked about using my credit card to pay for the car and was told that it could be arranged. The frequent flyer mileage would be enough to pay for our flight to Jill's graduation in May. Also since there were 2 years left on the Pontiac warranty, I said I did not want an extended warranty for $1995. Finally the manager called me into his office and printed out five sheets of papers for me to sign. He said I could use my credit card after I had taken out a loan with a bank in Philadelphia for 3 months. In a hurry to leave I signed the papers and departed, planning to have the car delivered to my house the next morning. I did not have the ownership paper on my van available when they delivered the car and said I would go through my file cabinet and bring it down the following day. as I had to leave for The play "Christmas Carol" in which I was participating. I told the manager about the extended warrantry that was still on the contract and he said he would have it cancelled. Not having carried and outstanding debts, since I retired, I didn't plan to start now so I called my mutual fund financial advisor and had him redeem 2 stock portfolios. With an anticipated 3 months to go before paying the bank, I decided to put the money in a 3 month CD. The day after making the deposit I received a coupon book from th PA bank listing 60 payments of $333.11 per month for 5 years and a total of $3,000 in interest. I immediately called them and explained the so called deal with the dealership. They said they did not take credit cards and I should discuss it with the dealer. I asked what the total would be if I paid immediately and they gave me that figure. Going to my bank, I cancelled the CD at a penalty of $95 and mailed a check for the balance which included $125 in interest. The $1995 was still included in the total so I called the Pittsfield owner of the car company from whom I had purchased my van 10 years ago, and who was my golf partner in the Senior League a few years ago, and explained the situation to him. He said he was going down to GT. Barrington that day and would talk to the sales manager about the warrant deal. Later I received a call saying it had been cancelled and I would be notified when the check was received. That call was not received. A few weeks later, I received a letter from the PA bank which included a check for $1995. The shoddy management in Gt. Barrington had sent the check to them instead of to me as promised. Luckily the bank was honest enough to sign the check and forward it to me.

In the Spring of 2008, Rosemary and I went to the annual Retired Senior Volunteer Persons, RSVP, appreciation luncheon at the Crown Plazza Hotel in Pittsfield, and were shocked to discover that we had been selected as volunteers of the year. We have both served terms as board members and in many other capacities. I video tape the program every year for community television and lead the pledge of allegiance and sing a patriotic song. Pictures of the awards by Mayor James Ruberto and Senator Ben Downing as well as family members in attendance are included. They were also in the RSVP calender for 2009, and we were part of the float for the 4th of July parade.

For 2009, Rosemary's sister, Eleanor Persip, was the winner. She has also participated in many community endeavors, especially the Pittsfield Senior Center where she has taught woodworking, and started a bridge club.

Grandaughter, Jillion Ashley Crawford, graduated with high honors from the University of Southern California in 2008 and did an internship with General Mills in Phoenix, Arizona for the summer. She had majored in Marketing and Philosophy. She was hired immediately and began demonstrating her marketing skills and attended several workshops and training sessions in other branches of the organization. This year she received a promotion.

Grandaughter, Vanessa Renee Smith, and her significant other, became the parents of a girl, Malia, last year, shortly after a shower and birthday celebration were held by the families of both sides in Nashua, New Hampshire. The baby was given the name of the father, Bruce Burgois, although no marriage plans are contemplated. It is ironic that all four of our great grandchildren are illegimate. That seems to be the trend of the younger generation these days, and will make genealogical history more difficult in the future.

At the family reunion in Maryland in July, Peter and Helen Dove Crawford were honored for their 60th wedding anniversary. This reunion was hosted by their daughter, Cheryl and her husband, Frank Nelson at the Comfort Inn in Beltsville, Maryland. With the Stout families living nearby there was a large attendence. Present for the first time were Charles Edward Crawford, Jr. his wife Raeshell Bogard and their two sons, Ryan and Devin.

The Stouts will host the reunion for 2010.

Well, thats the end of my story. Not knowing how many days, weeks, months, or years I have left on this earth, I give thanks to God for all his many benefits and the enrichment of life that I have received over the years despite the obstacles and mishaps.

Politics

My voting started in 1948 after finishing college and settling in the Berkshires. I registered as an independent voter and have remained so for the past 61 years, voting for the candidate whom I perceive as the most qualified to work for the benefit of the country and not just for special interests. Both parties have deteriorated in that regard over the years. Southern Democrats like George Wallace, Strom Thurmond, and Lyndon Johnson expressed their opposition to equal rights for minorities in order to maintain votes and remain in office, until the situation started changing in the 1960's and Wallace and Johnson did an about face. As president, Johnson even endorsed the new Civil Rights bill and took credit for its passage.

Republicans were leaders in the Northeast and midwest. and began catering to special interest lobbies who made contributions to their campaigns.

As the years rolled by party membership began a dramatic shift as Republicans took over the Southern states which endorsed their far right conservative religious trickle down economy and maintained most of the west. Democrats, supposedly with the best interests for the poor and middle class became more liberal and concerned about the country and economy as a whole.

Seeing where the country was headed Barack Obama won a decisive victory over his opponent, John McCain. With his optimism for change and many new ideas, he captured the votes of many young people, minorities and the poor. But his first year in office as the first so called "Black" President has been beset with unbelievable criticism and attacks by Republicans and a few Democrats whose primary purpose is to prevent positive changes by false accusations and media attacks to undermine public opinion and to protect and increase their seats in the Senate and the House of Representatives.

Wall Street is doing its best to prevent a speedy recovery by buying stocks when the prices are low and selling them off when the prices rise causing a see-saw up and down market. The bail out for the Auto industry and for banks still resulted in hugh layoffs and closing of plants.

Manufacturing has continued to be shipped overseas and most of the clothes, appliances and electronic devices have the label of an Asian Country, especially China. Here at home the jobless rate has been rising for most of the year, 2009, resulting in more home foreclosures, food banks, meals for the homeless and increased criminal activity by desperate people.

It appears that the health care bill will pass in the Senate, but unfortunately, with compromises and watered down objectives that benefit certain senators in order to insure their vote.

Probably this country will never see a united legislature body interested in what is best for the country as a whole; but, obviously, the present self service system will not work.

The Crawford Family Album

Isaac with Nellie and Tillie on Farm

Crawford family picture, Great Barrington, MA in 1946
standing in back from left: Ruth Mary, Peter Frank, Pearl Emily,
Isaac, Jr., and twins, Marie and Jerry: Seated; Martha holding Charles,
Edward and Isaac, Sr.

Isaac, Jr. shoveling snow in Normal IL

Martha Jane Wright and Isaac Crawford, Sr. wedding picture

President John Ostresh and Isaac Crawford, vice president
Dalton Community TV Board

Cutting the cake

August 24, 1947 Wedding of Rosemary Persip and Isaac
Crawford, Jr.

Marie's wedding to J. Alvin Stout, Jr. 1950

Ruth's graduation as a Registered Nurse from
St. Lukes School of Nursing

Ruth Crawford and husband, Tommy Evans

Cheshire Elementary Home Room Class

Annual meeting

Baked Salmon

50 years plus of membership at First Baptist Church

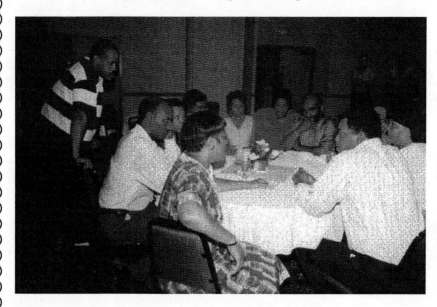

Grandchildren discuss family reunion plans

Martha Crawford honored on 30th anniversary of Macedonia
Baptist Church

Tuskegee Alumni class of 1948 honored on 50th Anniversary,1998

Receiving the 50th anniversary class award from Dr. Benjamin F. Payton
President of Tuskegee University

Charles Edward Crawford, Jr. and new bride, Raeshell Bogard

Family home site

Jill's graduation

Rosemary and Isaac receiving RSVP volunteers of the year
award from Mayor James Roberto at annual Awards
Luncheon in May 2008

Pearl and Isaac after graduation from Elementary School

Peter and Isaac, Jr. in Bearfork with 2 dogs

Martha and Isaac Sr. celebrate 55 years of marriage

30th anniversary

Rosemary and Isaac swim at Pontusuc Lake

My office in new log cabin home

Teaching Related Theory in Culinary Arts at McCann Tech 1969.

Rosemary's mother, Augusta Price Persip, father Alfred Persip
and Sister, Eleanor Persip.

Cousins at 50th anniversary

Persips and Crawfords in formal attire

President of Tabcom, 1990-1992

11 year volunteer, Isaac, Jr., standing by a photo of Congressman Silvio
Conte for whom the National Archives branch in Pittsfield was named

Cousins at reception after Aunt Irma's funeral

Golfer Ike at Wahconah Country Club

Listen my people and you shall hear,
about the birthday of a man so dear.
Twas the twenty-fifth of June, in twenty-four
when this man was born, so close to the kitchen floor.
He's flown, he's cooked, he's fought in war,
he's taught, he's sung, and does so much more.

Cable TV, Ike's Forum and golf,
gardening, computers, bowling and golf.
Church, family, community and golf,
father, husband, grandfather and golf.

Ike is his name, but golf is his game!

So listen my children and you shall hear,
about the birthday of this man so dear.
Born in "Normal" in twenty-four,
he had no idea what life had in store.

Working the farm and hunting bare foot,
Whistler and Chehaw, heard on the train with soot.
"Alley Bammy Bound", Tuskegee he found,
but World War 2 took him from that ground.

Trained in Great Lakes, he showed what it takes,
sent to Treasure Island, with the Pacific on the make.
With rhyme and cards, he set out to sea,
with the Navy, the "Japs", and his APD.

We're glad he prevailed through that time of war,
with his life and stories which we both adore.

So listen my children, and you shall hear
how Ike met Rosemary, that's why we are here.
Visiting the family, dancing having fun,
he met the girl that he knew was the one.

Married in that day's hottest sun,
they headed to New York to have some fun.
Lightening struck their hotel that night,
letting them know, that life would be all right!

In forty-eight he had a daughter so great,
looking so good, was it "puds" or "cakes"?
She was "the one" until almost eight,
when along came a son, making four on that date.

So listen my children and you shall hear,
about the birthday of this man so dear.
Currently in "Dalton" celebrating Seventy-four,
living life to the fullest, reaching for much more.

Our love for dad is neither hot nor cold,
our love for dad is with heart and soul.
So listen my father and you shall hear,
how much your family, loves you so dear.

HAPPY BIRTHDAY !!!!!!!!!! Happy 74th

poem sent to me on my 74th Birthday in 1998
by son Isaac Allen

Holiday Dinners in Gt. Barrington with Martha and Isaac, Sr

Singing christmas Carol

Martha with Grandchildren

On Lakeway drive

Berkshire Eagle Pictures

1943,New recruit at Camp Robert Small, Great Lakes, IL

1946, Going home on Patrol Gunbot Mechanized PGM 129

Peter Crawford, Sr, Brother Isaac and 2 daughters
not identified; early 1900s

Student Martha Jane Wright, second seated on left
Moody Bible School in Chicago

Maternal Grandparents: Frank and Emma Duncan Wright
son Edward and daughter Irma. Baby may be Peter

Alfred and Charles Persip Veterans Day Parade
Oct. 28, 1974
Both were WWI Veterans

Isaac Crawford Jr.

Church layman speaks Sunday

NORTH ADAMS—Isaac Crawford Jr., of Dalton, will be the Brotherhood Sunday speaker at the First Baptist Church's 9:30 a.m. worship service this Sunday. His topic will be "Involvement: A Christian Challenge."

Mr. Crawford, who is best known in northern Berkshire as coordinator of food services at McCann School, is known in the Pittsfield area as an active member and former chairman of the board of deacons of the First Baptist Church and moderator of the Berkshire Baptist Association. He is vice president of the Christian Center, treasurer of Partners in Progress and of the Minority Council on Community Concerns, and a former member of the Pittsfield Code of Enforcement Commission and the Berkshire Lyric Theater. He also is a vice president of the Northern Berkshire Chapter of the National Conference of Christians and Jews.

He graduated from Tuskegee Institute, Alabama, with a B.S. in Food Administration in 1948, and received his master's degree in education from North Adams State College in 1968. He taught fifth and sixth grade geography and sixth grade English at the Cheshire Elementary School in 1967-68, and was a chef and caterer for many years prior to entering the teaching field.

Craig F. Walker
Isaac Crawford Jr.

Crawford heads Massachusetts Baptist group

PITTSFIELD — Isaac Crawford Jr., a member of the First Baptist Church of Pittsfield, was elected president of the American Baptist Churches of Massachusetts at the annual meeting in Boston on April 27.

He succeeds the Rev. Dale Lock, pastor of First Baptist, who completed two terms in that office.

Crawford received a bachelor's degree in food administration from Tuskegee (Ala.) Institute and a master's degree in education from North Adams State College.

He is a former chairman of the culinary arts department at McCann Technical School, a position from which he retired in 1989. He is also a former president of the McCann Faculty Association.

He is certified in elementary education, occupational education, special education and teaching with computers, as well as being certified as an executive chef and culinary educator by the American Culinary Federation.

A member of the boards of directors of the Berkshire Chapter of the American Red Cross and the American Culinary Federation, Crawford is a member of First Baptist's Chancel and Cantata Choirs and has served on the diaconate board of trustees and nominating committee. He is a past moderator of the Berkshire Baptist Association and a past second vice president of the American Baptist Churches of Massachusetts.

He and his wife, Rosemary, live in Dalton. They have two children and four grandchildren.

Isaac Crawford Jr. Named To Code Enforcement Board

Mayor Del Gallo today appointed Isaac Crawford Jr. of 41 Lakeway Drive to the Code Enforcement Commission.

Crawford will represent people who live in areas where there is a high instance of substandard housing. The commission is charged with the task of eliminating substandard housing in Pittsfield by 1975.

By appointing Crawford, Del Gallo is making a concession to neighborhood action groups and the Pittsfield Council of Church-es, which argued that the citizens living in the target areas should have representation on the board.

Del Gallo had hand-picked the commission to include only city officials who had technical skills in fields related to the task of upgrading housing in Pittsfield.

The appointment will be up for City Council approval at a meeting Tuesday.

Crawford, 42, is a native of Normal, Ill. He now is employed at the Log Cabin Restaurant in Lenox.

He holds a bachelor of science degree in food administration from Tuskegee (Ala.) Institute, and now is working toward a master's degree from North Adams State College.

He came to Pittsfield in 1948. He is married to the former Rosemary Persip, who is a registered nurse at St. Luke's Hospital. They have two children.

Crawford is a member of the Organization for Community Action, and is a deacon of the First Baptist Church.

Association names Isaac Crawford Jr. 'Chef of the Year'

Isaac Crawford, department chairman in culinary arts at McCann Technical School in North Adams, was named "Chef of the Year" by the Berkshire Chefs' Association, the local chapter of the American Culinary Federation, at a recent dinner at the Gateways Inn in Lenox.

Winners are listed in the National Culinary Review. First Berkshire recipient was Roger Bismore, who founded the chapter. Formerly executive chef at the Williams Inn, Williamstown, he now is executive chef at The Old Tavern in Grafton, Vt., where he started another chapter, the Southern Vermont Chefs and Cooks Association.

Currently Berkshire chapter president, Mr. Crawford was treasurer for two years after the organization was formed. He edits the monthly newsletter, maintains the membership directory and keeps the financial records. He attended the federation's annual convention last summer in Sacramento, Calif., will attend the northeast regional conference in Philadelphia, Pa., in April, and the national meeting in Phoenix, Ariz., next summer.

At McCann, Mr. Crawford also teaches related theory in the classroom and supervises the school lunch program. He instituted the annual gourmet dinner to give students an opportunity to demonstrate their talents and raise funds for activities and field trips. His students have participated in the chapter's two culinary salons and plan to par-

AWARD PRESENTATION—Terrence Flynn, president of the Teacher's Association at Charles H. McCann Technical School, second from left, presents Issac Crawford Jr., second from right, with the Distinguished Vocational Teacher Award. Looking on are Barbara Cheesbro, treasurer, and William Fuhrmann, vice president. (Transcript-Anne Levesque)

Peers honor work of Crawford

NORTH ADAMS — Issac Crawford Jr., the culinary arts department chairperson at Charles H. McCann Technical School, was honored Monday by the McCann Faculty Association MFA president.

Terrence Flynn, presented a Distinguished Vocational Teacher award to Crawford at the MFA's March Meeting. The award was given during Vocational Technical Education Week (March 12-18) to highlight the role of teachers in Vocational Technical Education, according to Flynn.

Crawford has taught culinary arts theory at McCann since 1968. He also serves as food services director, managing the school's hot lunch and breakfast program.

Crawford is a charter member of the McCann Faculty Association and has been very active in its affairs. He has served as president and vice president of the MFA and chairperson of its negotiations committee.

The award acclaiming Crawford as a Distinguished Vocational Teacher cited him as "A man of the highest personal and professional integrity who...devoted his considerable gifts to the education of students, to the good of the school...(and) has been a dedicated and productive member of the McCann Faculty Association."

Crawford will be retiring at the end of the current school year.

Obituaries and Funerals

Martha Crawford, former caterer

PITTSFIELD — Mrs. Martha Crawford, 86, of 46 Lanark Road, who had lived and operated businesses in Great Barrington for many years, died Tuesday evening at Springside Nursing Home, where she had been a patient for three weeks.

She was owner and operator of the former Crawford's Inn & Catering Service and Crawford Employment Bureau in Great Barrington, a former food service supervisor at Lee High School and a midwife. She retired in 1972.

Mrs. Crawford was born July 26, 1902, in Mobile, Ala., the daughter of Frank and Emma Duncan Wright. She lived in Great Barrington from 1942 until the death of her husband, Isaac Crawford Sr., on March 7, 1978, after 56 years of marriage. They were married Oct. 1, 1921.

She was instrumental in organizing the Macedonia Baptist Church in Great Barrington, where she had taught Sunday school and was president of the Missionary Society. She also was a past matron of the Beulah chapter, Order of the Eastern Star, a former member of the Berkshire Baptist Association and past president of the Woman's League of First Baptist Church.

She leaves four sons. Isaac Crawford Jr. of Dalton, Peter F. Crawford of Boston, Dr. Jerry Crawford of Bloomfield, Conn., and Charles E. Crawford of Pittsfield; two daughters, Mrs. Ruth Evans of Pittsfield, with whom she made her home, and Mrs. Marie Stout of Monmouth Junction, N.J.; a brother, Joseph Wright of Vallejo, Calif.; a sister, Mrs. Irma Caleb of Mobile; 22 grandchildren; 20 great-grandchildren, and a great-great-grandchild.

The funeral will be Saturday at 11 at the First Baptist Church. Burial will be in Elmwood Cemetery, Great Barrington.

Calling hours at the Dery Funeral Home will be tomorrow from 2 to 4 and 7 to 9.

In lieu of flowers, memorial donations may be made to the Macedonia Baptist Church in care of the funeral home.

Boldyga, Alexander Z. 'Leo'
Clarke, Francis J.
Crawford, Martha Wright
Finizola, John A.
Hughes, Marie Verchot
Lund, Helene Leach
McCarty, Blanche Gerard
Simeno, Anna Anderson
Tower, Elizabeth Carstatter
Winchell, Daniel H.

Martha Crawford

The funeral of Mrs. Martha Wright Crawford of Pittsfield was Saturday at First Baptist Church in Pittsfield. The Rev. James Chase, a close friend of the family, officiated, and was assisted by the Rev. Joseph Forte, pastor of Macedonia Baptist Church in Great Barrington. Burial was in Elmwood Cemetery, Great Barrington.

Bearers were Isaac Crawford Jr. and Peter F., Jerry and Charles E. Crawford, sons; Alvin Stout, a son-in-law, and Richard Brinson, a grandson.

Martha Crawford, former owner of Barrington inn

PITTSFIELD — Martha Crawford, 86, of 46 Lanark Road, the retired owner of Crawford's Inn and Catering Service of Great Barrington, died on Tuesday in a local nursing home.

She was also a food service supervisor at Lee High School, and retired in 1972.

Born in Mobile, Ala., she lived in Great Barrington from 1942 to 1978.

She was instrumental in organizing the Macedonia Baptist Church, and was active in the Berkshire Baptist Association.

She was a past matron of the Beulah chapter of the Order of Eastern Star. She also taught Sunday School in Great Barrington, and served as a midwife.

Her husband, Isaac Crawford, died in 1978.

She leaves four sons, Isaac Jr. of Dalton, Peter F. of Boston, Dr. Jerry of Bloomfield, Conn., and Charles E. of Pittsfield; two daughters, Ruth Evans of Pittsfield, with whom she lived, and Marie Stout of Monmouth Junction, N.J.; a brother, Joseph Wright of Vallejo, Calif.; a sister, Irma Caleb of Mobile; 22 grandchildren; 20 great-grandchildren, and a great-great-grandchild.

The funeral will be Saturday morning in First Baptist Church, with burial in Elmwood Cemetery, Great Barrington. Dery Funeral Home is in charge.

Calling hours will be Friday.

Memorial contributions may be made to the Macedonia Baptist Church.

When in doubt, read the directions

The Crawfords build a prefab log home in Dalton

By BARBARA VAN NICE

Isaac Crawford's house might have been chosen out of the now-defunct Whole Earth Catalogue, but it wasn't.

It was out of a newer catalogue from a blossoming industry, the build-your-own-log-home business.

With his son, wife, daughter, a hired carpenter, and "a little help from assorted friends and relatives who passed by," Crawford three years ago assembled what appeared to be oversized Lincoln-logs, children's playthings, into a six-room, one-floor plus basement home.

Illinois original

"It's a little different from typical New England style," says Crawford, ironically an Illinois native who moved to Great Barrington in the late 1940s. Now a teacher and supervisor of food services at McCann Regional Vocational School in North Adams, he lives in Dalton.

From mid-summer to late fall in 1969, construction of the house drew onlookers to the one-acre site in the pine woods on Kirchner Road.

Some people asked for guided tours—and received them. "Even the Dalton police stopped to watch," Crawford says. At one point, friends suggested the family charge tourist fees.

Even now, three years later, people driving past sometimes ogle. "A lot of them stop and look and slowly drive on." Crawford says, chuckling, but with some pride. "Even had a couple of contractors come out."

Insulated by nature

"Did you expect to see mud chinks?" Crawford asked the reporter, apparently reading her mind as it recalled the log cabin pictures of pioneer and backwoods tales.

In this age of pre-fabricated everything, though, there are, in fact, no mud chinks. Tongue and groove notches on the logs lock together when slammed by a sledgehammer, which is how Crawford and helpers spent long hours that summer. The joint thus forms a solid wall of wood, which acts as insulation.

With few m i s t a k e s and equally few injuries—inflamed wrist ligaments and a slightly battered finger—Crawford persevered. "I was up there (on the roof) some nights pounding nails after school," he says.

Before deciding on the house plan, which comes in about a dozen models, "I spent all day

Isaac Crawford

with a fellow in Vermont" where a number of similar houses are up. A McCann librarian had first introduced him to the idea.

However, at that point, "I told them (the firm) to hold it 'til I had somewhere to put it," he says. The family bought the Dalton site, moved from their Lakeway Drive home in Pittsfield, and settled into an apartment while construction was in progress.

It took about two months to obtain a building permit, Crawford says, because the inspector, who was unfamiliar with the plan or construction methods, wanted to be sure the house would stay up.

Western cedar logs

"They tell me some of these are still standing after 200 years," he adds in a gently mocking tone, apparently recalling those pioneer log cabins. His modern equivalent was the first in the Pittsfield-Dalton area, he believes, though there are others elsewhere in the county.

After a delay, the western cedar pieces were delivered by freight car to the town from the West Coast and were hauled by truck to the site. There the family sorted out the stacks.

Like "easy-to-assemble" toys, only blueprints and stenciled

ent or unique," Crawford says of building a log home. "What excited me was the possibility of doing it myself . . . . I've always been willing to stick my neck out. I like a challenge."

Lumber alone cost $8,000 and freight added another $700 or $800, he says. Not to mention contracting costs for foundation-pouring, wiring (which requires holes to be drilled through the solid logs), plumbing, or masonry. "It all adds up," he says.

Besides the doing-your-own-thing aspect and the ability to make design changes, as Crawford did to enlarge bedroom closet and bathroom space, what are the advantages?

Cathedral ceilings

"With a house full of (cigarette) smoke, at least you can breathe" with the ceiling reaching to the roof beams, says Crawford.

"I like it because it's easy to clean, for one thing," says Mrs. Crawford, due to the varnished walls.

"No constant painting and papering to be done," adds Crawford.

However, there is still work to be done. Crawford planned to finish the basement, which has a fireplace of fieldstones from the yard, next summer, but the job will probably be delayed, he says.

The first summer he landscaped the yard. The second, he built the tool shed. The third, he

The Crawfords' log home living room.

set up the garage. At some point, too, a doghouse was made from the Lincoln-log remains.

Settled in and at home, the family proudly displays the photo album filled with pictures from various stages of construction.

Living in the house "took a while to get used to, but I like it," says Mrs. Crawford. Following advice to offset what some call the darkness and dreariness of log home interiors, the Crawfords have decorated in bright colors. Rich blue carpeting, an ochre sofa and floral-patterned curtains warm the living room.

Asked whether he is encouraging others to build log homes, Crawford answers, "Not directly." But, he adds, "I'm not discouraging them."

Other Class Members

Great Barrington's member of the nursing group is Miss Ruth Mary Crawford, daughter of Mr. and Mrs. Isaac Crawford of 14 Elm Court. She studied at Bennett College in Greensboro, N.C., for one year.

Although she comes all the way from Detroit, Miss Helen Ann Norwood has Pittsfield connections, since her grandmother, Mrs. Elizabeth Fry, lives at 147 John Street. Miss Norwood is also the cousin of Miss Morehead, the second-year student. Miss Norwood studied for two years at Marygrove College, a Catholic school of sisters in her home town.

Down-county people may recall Miss Brookie Mary Robinson, daughter of Mr. and Mrs. Willy Robinson of Birmingham, Ala. Miss Robinson worked for Dr. and Mrs. Richard M. Stevens, Stockbridge dentist, for a year. Before that she studied one year at Talladiga (Ala.) College.

Being a Catholic is not a requirement at the St. Luke's Hospital School of Nursing, although most of the students are of that faith. Miss Norwood has been a Catholic all along, while Miss Morehead was converted last year and Miss Robinson was converted recently.

Qualifications Explained

Qualifications for Pittsfield's two nursing schools are about the same. One exception is the Pittsfield General's Bishop Memorial School for Nurses, where no male students are allowed. St. Luke's, on the other hand, has two male students this year, the school's first in 10 years.

Both schools select their students on the basis of intelligence and aptitude. All students must obtain "satisfactory marks" on their pre-entrance nursing aptitude test supplied by the National League of Nursing Education. And both schools prefer girls who were in the upper half of their high school class.

"But," as Miss Mildred E. Schwier, director of nursing at the Pittsfield General, said, "we will take a girl who is in the lower bracket if her pre-entrance test and five references indicate she may do well."

Somewhat the same stipulation is made by Sister Mary Vincenti, director of nursing at St. Luke's. "We prefer those in the upper half of the high school class, but here are exceptions. For instance, if a girl had to do outside work while in school we assume that would leave her less time for studying, and therefore are willing to allow lower school marks in her case."

Both schools also give a rigid health examination and personal interviews are used to check on other qualities of the student. In addition, all girls must be approved by a committee on admissions.

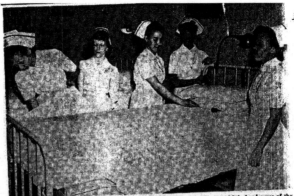

NEGRO TRAINEES MAKE BEDS: Miss Elsie Albareda, RN, second left, head nurse of the male surgical floor at St. Luke's Hospital, supervises bed-making class of four St. Luke's Negro trainees, among the first in Pittsfield history. The first one, Miss Elizabeth Morehead, who is in her second year, was absent when the picture was taken. Left to right, they are Miss Bronkie Mary Robinson of Birmingham, Ala.; Miss Helen Ann Norwood of Detroit, Mich.; Miss Nomina Chadwell, daughter of Mr. and Mrs. Leslie Chadwell of 41 Deering Street; and Miss Ruth Mary Crawford, daughter of Mr. and Mrs. Isaac Crawford of Great Barrington.

St. Luke's Negro Nurse Trainees
First in Local Hospital History

St. Luke's Hospital has the only group of Negro girls ever to take nursing training in Pittsfield.

Two From Pittsfield

Two of the five girls are from Pittsfield, one is from Great Barrington, and the other two are from Alabama and Michigan. Miss Elizabeth Morehead, daughter of Mrs. Lloyd Morehead of 147 John Street, is in her second year. She is the sister of Don Morehead, Pittsfield's High School's football and basketball star.

The other four girls were capped Sunday night at the completion of their six-month pre-clinical period. The Pittsfield girl in that group is Miss Nomina Chadwell, daughter of Mr. and Mrs. Leslie Chadwell of 41 Deering Street.

BERKSHIRE EVENING EAGLE
AUG 23 1952

Ruth M. Crawford Becomes Bride of Pittsfield Man

GREAT BARRINGTON — Ruth Mary Crawford, daughter of Mr. and Mrs. Isaac Crawford Sr. of Elm Court, was wed Saturday evening at 6 in a double-ring ceremony at the home of her parents, to Thomas Evans, son of Mr. and Mrs. Charles Evans of Pittsfield.

Rev. Herbert J. Murray Jr., assistant pastor of the First Baptist Church, Pittsfield, officiated in a garden decorated with gladioli roses and laurel leaves. Soloist was Miss Dolores Allen Freeman, who was accompanied by Professor Fernard Barrette.

The bride, given in marriage by her father, was attired in an ankle-length, off-the-shoulder gown of white organza with fitted bodice and skirt of three tiers edged with Chantilly lace and a matching lace-trimmed jacket. Her veil of nylon tulle and Chantilly lace was attached to a crown of pearl beads and rhinestones. She carried a Colonial bouquet of white roses with streamers of baby's-breath.

Mrs. Peter Crawford of Boston, sister-in-law of the bride, was matron of honor, and Rose Mary Crawford, niece of the bride, flower girl. Mrs. Crawford wore a mint green ballerina gown of net over taffeta with matching hat. She carried a Colonial bouquet of yellow roses with streamers of violets. The flower girl was dressed in yellow organdy with matching headpiece. She carried a basket of flowers.

William F. Evans, brother of the bridegroom, was best man. Ushers were Daniel B. Jones of this town and Samuel Stevenson of Pittsfield.

The mother of the bride wore a lavender crepe dress with gray accessories and pink rose corsage. The mother of the bridegroom chose a lime suit with matching accessories and a corsage of pink roses.

For her wedding trip to Ohio and Detroit, the bride chose a gray suit with black accessories and a corsage of red roses. The couple plan to make their home in Pittsfield.

A reception was held after the wedding at the home of the bride. Out-of-town guests were Mr. and Mrs. Thomas Bragg of Chicago, uncle and aunt of the bride, and Mrs. Herbert Whighan and son Harold Whighan, and Mrs. Betty Morris of Montclair, N.J.

Local Girl Passes Test for Nurses

Miss Ruth Mary Crawford

GREAT BARRINGTON — Miss Ruth Mary Crawford, daughter of Mr. and Mrs. Isaac Crawford of Elm Court, has passed the state examination for registered nurses.

A 1946 Searles High graduate, Miss Crawford attended Bennett College, Greensboro, N.C., and graduated from St. Luke's Hospital School of Nursing in Pittsfield last year. She is now on the staff at St. Luke's.

Dr. Crawford Opens Office In Hartford

Dr. Jerry Crawford

GREAT BARRINGTON — Dr. Jerry Crawford, son of Mr. and Mrs. Isaac Crawford Sr. of Elm Court, recently opened an office for the practice of internal medicine in Hartford, Conn.

A 1948 graduate of Searles High, Dr. Crawford received a B.S. degree from the Agricultural & Technical College of North Carolina and his M.D. degree from Howard University, College of Medicine, in Washington, D.C., in 1959.

Heart Assn. Fellowship

He served his internship at St. Francis Hospital in Hartford and underwent three years of specialty training there. He was recently awarded a fellowship by the Hartford Heart Association to continue part-time study and research with the St. Francis Hospital Cardiovascular Section, with which he has been associated for the past six months.

A two - year Army veteran, he served in the Korean War as an infantry officer. He is married to the former Gladys Lewis of Pittsfield. Among his brothers and sisters are two Pittsfield residents, Mrs. Ruth Evans of Lanark Road and Isaac Crawford Jr. of Lakeway Drive.

BECOMES DOCTOR

JERRY CRAWFORD

Mr. Crawford, son of Mr. and Mrs. Isaac Crawford, of Elm court received a doctor of medicine degree from Howard University School of Medicine in Washington D. C., this month. He will intern at St. Francis Hospital in Hartford, Conn., starting in July.

'BLACK' 1996

"The greatest threat to your health and longevity is your social behavior. Included in this is failure to put your health as top priority. the miracles of modern day science are meaningless if you do not take advantage of them before it's too late, or if you live a life of reckless abandon."

JERRY CRAWFORD, M.D.

"Many people think I must have been an only child," says Jerry Crawford. Actually, he came from a family of seven children, six are still living, including a twin sister. Encouraged by his mother since childhood, Dr. Crawford carefully prepared himself educationally for his chosen profession every step of the way. After successfully completing college and military service, it was quite logical for Jerry to begin the practice of medicine in a community that could use his skills and knowledge.

There are several reasons why Dr. Crawford chose Hartford to begin his practice. In 1959, the demographics of New England cities suggested Hartford as the area that had the most stability and potential for growth and a rapidly expanding minority population. Further, Hartford was close to Jerry's home in Western Massachusetts.

From the beginning Jerry Crawford has been a Primary Care and Internal Medicine physician. Since 1963 he has served as Assistant Visiting Physician in Medicine at the St. Francis Hospital and Medical Center. His education includes a B.S. degree from North Carolina A & T University, and an M.D. from Howard university College of Medicine.

Jerry believes he has had few, if any, great challenges during his career, once he completed medical school and decided where and in what field he would practice. However, professionally he is very aware of the small but important daily challenges of patient care: establishing a rapport; and making proper diagnoses and effective therapeutic plans.

Dr. Crawford considers his major achievement to be the continued uninterrupted solo practice of medicine for 33 years, and the thousands of people who gave him the chance to make a difference in their lives. Above all Jerry feels it a privilege to be viewed by thousands of families as a friend, trusted family member, health advisor, and "their doctor." Dr. Crawford says, "I still enjoy what I do and have no regrets."

Edwards Brothers,Inc!
Thorofare, NJ 08086
14 June, 2010
BA2010165